MW00899526

WELCOME TO THE GRIND

How Educators Achieve Exponential Results

Personalized PD
Used Pinterest-Twitter-Instagram To Earn Grad Credit
Register: Bitly.com/PPD_1

Randall G. Sampson

Welcome To The Grind!

Building Sustainable and Exponential Results

EST.1983

Dedication

Love asks me know no questions, and gives me endless support...
William Shakespeare

This book is dedicated to several people who have had a major impact in my writing a manuscript that will support educators for years to come.

First, quality is not possible without strong family support, love and faith. For buying into my dreams and unselfishly giving up their family time, I dedicate this book to my lovely wife Allison and my beautiful daughters Kalista, Sophia, and Hadley.

Secondly, there are friends who support your dreams and never hesitate to provide advice. Tom and Michelle Herman thank you for holding that honor.

Thirdly, throughout all areas of education, experts are needed to develop and share captivating stories that attract educators. As such, I am thankful for the deep-rooted friendship and knowledge of the contributing authors, and their kindness to share their experience in The Grind. I am forever grateful for their knowledge: Carolyn Hunter Rogers, Tyrone Olverson, Thomas Tucker, Mark Raiff, Jason Bates, Scott Cunningham, Steven McGhee, Derek Oldfield, Zach Peterson, Melissa Eddington, Vrondelia "Ronni" Chandler, Sean Ross, and Daryl Woodard.

Finally, no project is ever successful without those folk behind the scene. I am blessed to have a sanctuary of family and friends who support my vision and provide the words of encouragement for my endless projects.

CONTENTS

"Our Culture Defines Who We Are!"

THE AUTHOR

Randall G. Sampson (PhD) is the founder and chief executive officer of the Liberty Leadership Development Center. He has been a teacher and public school administrator, as well as a university professor and national transformation specialist. He is nationally acclaimed for his urban, suburban, and rural schools innovation. His philosophy ensures equity and access for students through personalized Blended Learning, Competency-Based, and Student-Centered models. Sampson honed many of his instructional and leadership skills through the Harvard University Achievement Gap Initiative and through teacher quality research with Harvard University's Ronald F. Ferguson. As a practitioner, Sampson's analysis of students' performance data provided a national value-add approach to building sustainable learning environments. Sampson's prior administrative work at Westerville North High School provided opportunities that allowed him to identify gaps in student enrollment in Advanced Placement (AP) courses. As such, the school district created systemic corrective measures to improve students' learning outcomes. As a result, the school experienced a 600% increase of African-American students enrolled in Advance Placement courses. Additionally, the school saw a 35% increase of students' AP exam scores rising from 3 to 4.

THE CONTRIBUTING AUTHORS

Thomas Tucker (PhD) served 26 years in the Kansas and Ohio public school systems. During that time, he held the positions of classroom teacher, assistant principal, principal, director of secondary curriculum and superintendent. Currently, Dr. Tucker serves as the superintendent of Princeton City Schools, Cincinnati, Ohio. Dr. Tucker was named the 2016 American Association of School Administrators (AASA) National Superintendent of the Year. In 2008, Dr. Tucker became not only the first African-American to be named superintendent of Licking Heights Local School District, but also earned the distinction of being the first African-American superintendent in Licking County. He is an active member of many educational associations, civic organizations and committees, including the Buckeye Association of School Administrators and the National Alliance of Black School Educators.

Carolyn Hunter Rogers (PhD) is the proud mother of two sons and two granddaughters. She has worked in P-12 and higher education for more than 40 years. She has served as teacher, co-ordinator, and principal and urban schools area superintendent in P-12 education. In higher education, she served as a faculty member, Chair of multiple departments (Educational Leadership, Special Education Leadership, and Curriculum and Instruction), and Associate Dean of the School of Education. Dr. Rogers is a dynamic visionary leader with countless skills that led her to open *Leadership Development Consulting* in 2002. As an educational consultant, Dr. Rogers worked with numerous P-12 teachers and administrators in raising the achievement and improvement of schools; and universities in evaluating grants. She is a people person and a master at building personal and strategic relationships. She understands that the establishment of solid relationships not only assists in furthering the goals and mission of the organization, it is the right thing to do. Dr. Rogers believes every child deserves an education that will ensure success for the future. In addition to numerous articles, Dr. Rogers co-authored *The Ten Commandments of Education*, a book specific for the caring teacher. Dr. Rogers believes teaching is a calling and an art! Educating children, teachers and leaders is her purpose in life. She lives by the motto, "Failure is not an Option!"

Mark Raiff serves as the superintendent of nationally acclaimed Olentangy Local School District. Raiff is a district resident and longtime administrator. Mr. Raiff begins his 28th year in education, having started his career in the Cleveland area in 1989 as a math, business and technology educator. After moving to central Ohio, Raiff served as administrator in Bexley City Schools and Westerville City Schools, before joining the Olentangy family in 2003. Raiff's leadership strengths include the characteristics that are integral to Olentangy's success. The district's vision for a community values excellence and building a respectful and caring environment in which high quality, research-based instruction is the ultimate goal. These traits, along with communication, collaboration and community support, are essential to the district's continued success.

Derek Oldfield is the assistant principal at Wirt County High School in Elizabeth, West Virginia. He lives in Parkersburg, WV with his wife, Julie, and five-year old daughter Miley. Oldfield has spent the last seven years teaching secondary mathematics. In the last four years his practices have shifted dramatically towards a standards-based, student-centered learning environment leveraging digital tools to improve outcomes. Oldfield taught in a 1:1 learning environment for the last two years and is now leading the learning of a 1:1 school at Wirt County High School. He is an advocate for empowerment and high expectations over compliance in the classroom. Oldfield is a lifelong learner leading a grassroots movement by connecting and supporting educators across the state of West Virginia. Since 2013, Mr. Oldfield has facilitated the #wvedchat Twitter community that meets, chats, supports, and learns together.

Jason Bates serves as assistant principal at Olentangy High School. He graduated from Ohio University in 2003 with a Bachelor's of Science Degree in Secondary Mathematics Education as well as a Bachelor's of Science degree in Mathematics. Bates began his teaching career at Groveport Madison Freshman Building for one year, before moving to Olentangy Orange Middle School. Bates taught 8th grade for five years and served as a team leader, department chair, and building leadership team. Bates was awarded the Olentangy Orange Middle School and Olentangy Local School District Teacher of the Year in 2008-2009. Bates then moved to Olentangy Orange High School where he taught Geometry inclusion, Honors Geometry, Honors Pre-Calculus and AP Calculus BC. In

2014, Bates accepted the Assistant Principal position at Olentangy High School. In this role, Bates is heavily involved with special education, professional development for staff, new teacher mentorship and instructional leadership.

Scott Cunningham is principal of Olentangy Orange Middle School in Ohio. He has over 18 years of experience in education as a principal, assistant principal, and teacher. Cunningham previously spent six years as principal at Prairie Norton Elementary School in the South-Western City School District. He led that school, which is ethnically diverse and has a high poverty rate, to a rating of "Excellent" on its state report card in 2011. Just 150 high-poverty schools in Ohio received that rating, the second-highest awarded.

Tyrone Olverson serves as Chief Academic Officer of Youngstown City Schools. Previously, Olverson served as superintendent of Finneytown Local School District in Ohio and former curriculum director in Licking Heights Local School District. Olverson is nationally renowned for his ability to build world-class school districts through the implementation of a Professional Learning Community process. The process served to increase teacher learning and improved student growth and achievement. During his tenure, Olverson has helped his districts increase Advanced Placement (AP) participation of all students in grades 9-12. This includes an overall AP participation increase of over 200%, including 40% of the 9th grade students taking an AP course. Olverson helped his district earned an Excellent 4-year Graduation Rate and 5-year

Graduation Rate from the Ohio Department of Education; "A" rating for Ohio Department of Education Standards Met; Overall Value-Added; and Gifted Value-Added.

Steven McGhee is the prior principal of Michigan's oldest high school, Detroit Central Collegiate Academy. Know by many as a change agent for public schools; he is a man of integrity and is extremely dedicated to his family, his career, and ALL children. After graduating from Henry Ford High School in Detroit in 1983, Steven returned to home to his birth state of Alabama to attend Alabama A&M University to earn his Bachelor of Science degree, Magna Cum Laude. He returned to Detroit, after a successful teaching career in Virginia, to instruct in Detroit Public Schools at Crockett Career and Technical Center. At this time he furthered his education by completing his Masters Degree in Administrative Leadership; Cum Laude in 1999 at Wayne State University. He has developed the first high school education/business consortium, which includes educational entities and non-profit organi--zations, offering services to promote student learning. Central also has a state of the art Cyber Café, writing lab, music/sound studio, broadcasting room, courtroom, technology room for filming lessons, and a parent resource room.

Zach Peterson serves as a Spanish Language Teacher and Boys Head Lacrosse Coach at Olentangy High School in Lewis Center, Ohio. He is passionate about growing leaders, developing curriculum, and impacting culture. Zach lives in the Lewis Center community with his wife Colleen, and their daughter Kennedy. In his free time, Zach enjoys coaching lacrosse, playing golf, and playing the guitar.

Melissa Eddington serves as an English as a Second Language educator in Dublin City Schools (DCS). Mrs. Eddington is currently in her 17th year of teaching, having started her career in the Logan-Hocking School District as a kindergarten teacher. After moving to central Ohio, Eddington continued her teacher career in Columbus City Schools before joining DCS in 2007. As a nationally connected leader, Eddington has helped educators personalize their instructional practices to better meet the needs of their students, families, and communities. At the local level, Mrs. Eddington continues to lead Dublin City Schools' collaborative #DubChat Twitter forum. She holds a bachelor degree in Elementary Education from Ohio Northern University, a Master in the Art of Teaching (MAT) from Marygrove College and an Educational Administration master's degree from Miami University. Eddington resides in Hilliard with her husband, Mike, daughter Genevieve, son Gabriel and various pets.

Vrondelia "Ronni"Chandler serves as the executive director and CEO of Project GRAD Knoxville, which focuses on increasing academic achievement, high school graduation rates and college-going and success rates for students from 14 of Knoxville's urban schools. Chandler has worked at Project GRAD Knoxville since its inception in 2001, first as a program director and now as executive director. Since Project GRAD Knoxville was founded in 2001, the graduation rate at Fulton and Austin-East high schools increased from about 50 percent to more than 80 percent. Approximately 57 percent of those students now go on to postsecondary education, and the completion rate for those students in higher education is 46 percent — far higher than the national average of 10 percent for students from low-income circumstances. Chandler is the recipient of the 2016 Pellissippi State Distinguished Alumni Award. This awards is bestowed upon an individual in recognition of significant professional achievement, service to the community and support of the College and the Pellissippi State Foundation. Chandler is both a graduate and former employee of Pellissippi State.

Sean M. Ross (PhD) joined PCA in 2013 as the Chief Operating Officer and Chief Learning Officer and is responsible for day to day oversight, leadership initiatives, program performance and growth in the areas of public service and collaborative leadership training and development. Dr. Ross has had an extensive and successful career in public education as a teacher, coach, and administrator. He developed and shaped individuals to reach beyond their potential and achieve lifelong success. As a leader in education, Ross was a key component in one of the most accomplished school districts in the nation and provided direction for student, teacher, and community achievements. He was an essential contributor to the schools being named as one the top districts in the country as ranked by US News & World Report. As a facilitator of leadership development, he has built strong collaborations with public safety, education and government agencies helping to foster growth by bridging relationships and building leadership.

Daryl M. Woodard is the founder of Wilson Preparatory Academy began with Daryl M. Woodard and his wife, Shawan Barfield Woodard. Daryl M. Woodard, founded his own non-profit, Smart Choices for Youth, Inc. (formerly Wayne County Youth Outreach) in 1989, managing federal, state and local grant funds focused on mentoring, after-school programming and improving academic and behavioral performance to thousands of youth for over 25 years. His wife, Shawan Woodard, a former middle school teacher, have served thousands of youth and families together since. Mr. and Mrs. Woodard researched a blended learning charter school concept to expand their services through the development of a new innovative, technology based college preparatory academy. This birthed the idea and implementation of Wilson Preparatory Academy.

THE OVERVIEW

Welcome To The Grind will document the six-pillars that nationally acclaimed contributing authors have identified as essential in building an elite culture for learning.

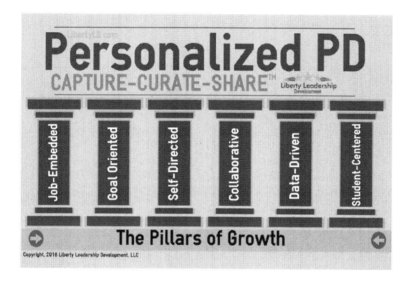

Job-Embedded process has an emphasis on the day-to-day act of learning and improving skills. Making the direct connection between learning and doing is critical in any Job-Embedded approach.

Goal Oriented process has clarity of focus on achievement and completion of task. Elite organizations develop goals to predict future success of task.

Self-Directed means having the autonomy to lead your personal growth.

Collaborative is the process of leveraging strengths and weakness in order to work together with a common purpose.

Data-Driven is the discipline to believe in the insights of experience and make decisions that are good for the team.

Student-Centered has a keen focus on the learners and their experiences.

Our Culture Defines Who We Are!
"Relationship x Process = Exponential Results"

Too often we believe that maximum effort is sufficient. In the GRIND you must have contingency plans and strategies when your effort doesn't take you in the direction you envisioned.

- The GRIND requires you to develop a grit mindset.
- The GRIND requires you to pay attention to the little things and align your goals with winning strategies.
- The GRIND requires you to focus on both the technical and adaptive changes, to win the day.

The GRIND comes down to creating a process of self-discipline and building a culture of relentless effort.

Winning doesn't happen in one defining moment; winning occurs when we make a choice to improve incrementally. This choice comes to us every day, often taking place multiple times per day. We have to move forward, beyond the comfort of the moment. Improvement requires a strong will to succeed every minute of the day.

The GRIND manifests itself in the form of both technical and adaptive change. Technical changes are those nuts and bolts adjustments required in any systemic process. Adaptive changes are those natural moments that occur on a more personalized relationship level. Once both sides of this equation are balanced, great results will be evident. Elite results are only visible if you have attainable processes, coupled with strong personal relationships.

"Culture defines who you are and how you prepare for pressure!"
-University of Texas, Coach Tom Herman

Welcome To The Grind deep dives the concepts of what it takes to be considered elite at your craft. From the onset, parallelism will be drawn from sports to culture. One does not have to be an elite athlete, nor a weekend warrior to understand the concept of increasing performance and building a strong team culture. Those organizations that focus on developing sustainable and exponential results typically focus on these points:

1. **Personalized growth of your people**

2. **Excitement about your dynamic process**

3. **Clarity of the organization's vision and mission**

Elite athletes and coaches have a clear understanding of the GRIND. Most people believe that physical competitiveness is the most critical component of athletics. However, elite athletes and coaches will tell you "once you reach an elite level, the hardest competition is between the ears."

Mental toughness and grit mindset drive the elite athletes through the finish line. The same goes for educators; a small segment of our general population can become elite teachers. The GRIND requires great teachers to pay attention to the little details of the learning and growing experience. Elite teachers have a grit mindset that challenges their self-improvement, effectiveness, and collective impact.

Professional growth and success come down to the individual's professional level of grit and willingness to embrace the GRIND. This same mentality has to transfer to the classroom and the student learning experience. Only 2 – 6% of high school students join the ranks of elite college athletes. In K-12 education, teachers are charged with teaching 100% of *all* students and to meet the established academic levels. This book will explore the stories of those educators who have mastered the art of the K-12 student learning experience. The task is not always easy, nor should it have to be. For those educators willing and able to go the extra yard for the success of their students, ***Welcome To The Grind!***

MY STORY

I had an opportunity to vacation and play a couple rounds of golf with The Ohio State University's 2014 College Football Playoff National Champion Offensive Coordinator and current University of Texas Head Coach, Tom Herman. We played golf the summer leading up to The Ohio State University Football team winning the 2014 National Championship. Both of our families were on vacation in South Carolina, and our daughters were on the same national dance competition team. Tom and I figured we could get a few rounds of golf in; oddly, our wives encouraged it. That was the first time Tom and I hung out, beyond the typical minivan car pool small talk.

I'm an Ohio State Alumnus and the first to admit, "Buckeye Nation" stays at a fevered pitch 24/7 about their football. The Ohio State University has an international alumni base of over 500,000 active members; the expectation of excellence from the football team is simply **HIGH**. The 2014 off-season hope was for All-American quarterback candidate Braxton Miller to lead the football team to the 2014 Big Ten Championship and earn an outside chance at making the first National Championship playoff.

Being a diehard Buckeye fan, I could talk football endlessly; I knew Tom probably wanted to distance himself from work and consume himself in vacation mode. I'm sure he was looking for a mental break with family time at the beach, splashing in the pool, and playing some golf. Knowing this was my opportune time to get the inside scoop on Buckeye football, but I suppressed my desire to talk football. I refused to be "that guy;" the ultimate destroyer of a well-deserved vacation. Plus, I was trying to shape up my pathetic golf game, and any little distractions would have quickly derailed me. So the golf game ensued along with a conversation that will forever change my mode of operation. Coach Herman's functional blueprint for maximizing human talent gave me a moment of pause and insight.

"Process x Relationship = Exponential Results"

When two guys are sitting hip-to-hip in a golf cart for eight hours in the scorching South Carolina summer heat, within the first hour, you can tell if you are going to enjoy the person's company. The early morning South Carolina humidity made us both wonder if this was going to be a long day. After the first tee shot, Tom and I clicked personality-wise. At least for me, that awkward "getting to know you" moment was not evident.

I was surprised that Tom wanted to talk about his personal coaching experiences. The conversation was not about specific football plays, strategies or personnel. The conversation was about the great relationships he had with staff, players, and families. Tom spoke from the heart about his football experiences which allowed him to develop authentic and meaningful relationship. I felt as if Tom was talking about his personal family. The passion and love for his players and colleagues oozed out of his pores.

When you hear people say "that's my brother from another mother," Tom has a way of making a person feel that comfortable. I started talking about my family and personal life, while Tom spoke openly and candidly about his life experiences. We were paired up with a couple of retired "snowbirds" from Pennsylvania. We could tell these two guys were the best of friends, as they heckled each other and engaged in constant laughter. I saw this look of envy and amazement in Tom's eyes and recall him saying, "One day, we will be like these old guys." The pure joy of deeply-rooted friendships and meaningful relationships are the core of Tom's being.

You can tell when someone is genuine about building authentic relationships because they have no agenda; they stay true to themselves. Typically, you would think that these high-level college football coaches will only tell recruits, families or fans what they want to hear. But, Tom was as genuine as it gets.

"In real estate, it's all about LOCATION, LOCATION, LOCATION; in education, it's all about RELATIONSHIP, RELATIONSHIP, RELATIONSHIP."

Parallel to coaching, in the education profession, you sink or swim based on your ability to build authentic relationships.

While golfing, I noticed Tom being a very unassuming person and very willing to soak up as much learning as possible. There was no hint of entitlement or ego, just a lifestyle of being inquisitive. As a certified Mensa International member, Tom never gave the vibe of being the smartest person in the room; in this case, the smartest person on the golf course. I asked Tom why he doesn't talk about his International Mensa certification? Without missing a beat, Tom replied, "that wouldn't help my duck-hook golf shot." Tom's humility is a refreshing experience, based on the hype of his position as an elite college football coach and certified Mensa member.

"A combination of humility and professional will"
- Jim Collins, Good to Great Level 5 Leadership

Tom also said something in passing, but it stuck with me, *"We are only as good as the recruits we bring in. We are only great if we emotionally invest in our players and develop their talents beyond what they thought was possible."* To the average person, this sounds like typical recruiting or car salesmen stuff, but he meant it. As we were golfing, Tom's attention to detail and preparation poured out of him under the hot South Carolina sun. After teeing off at the seventh hole, Tom said, "I noticed you are wearing cross-trainer shoes instead of golf shoes." I told him golf shoes are so uncomfortable and make my legs tired at the end of the round. He looked at me and said, "For years, I thought I was the only one with those issues… interesting!"

The next day when we played another round, Tom showed up with his Ohio State football cross-trainers on and a bounce in his step. Great leaders are always willing to learn and adapt their process, to be successful. But, most importantly Tom was looking for a way to improve his game, and he knew that having fresh legs in the smoldering South Carolina summer would help him tremendously. That day, Tom's golf game was on fire. He demonstrated humility by making slight adjustments for self-improvement, and the results were evident. This was a great leadership lesson for me; continuous learning is the conduit for improvement.

While we were golfing, I noticed that Tom was not looking to edge me out for a win. In the past, some guys that I had golfed with seem to constantly count and tally my strokes. I have learned that great leaders don't try to win by focusing on the competition; they win by improving themselves and their organization. Great leaders are hyper competitive with their development and their self-improvement.

"Control what you can control and the outcomes will follow."

Tom was so hyper-focused on improving his game that I couldn't get him off the golf course, even as a mid-day South Carolina summer lightning storm was brewing. The violent storm was forcing golfers to head for cover, but Tom's intense focus would not hear my call to run for shelter. He kept saying "we are ahead of the storm; let's play a few more holes." The fiery competitor was evident at that time. The competition was between his ears, not with the guy sitting next to him.

As I ran to pull Tom off the golf course, I had this flashback image of the classic golf movie Caddie Shack. As a loud boom of thunder shook our golf clubs and lighting danced above our heads, finally Tom said, "I think we better take cover." Needless to say we were lucky that day; we parked the golf cart under a tree canopy, while waiting out the storm. During the rain delay, he kept glaring at the scorecard and talked about each stroke and planning how to improve when we get out to the remaining holes. Tom insisted that we go back out as soon as the storm blew over. Our first soggy tee-shot was the indicator that we had to save it for another day. The golf balls were landing in the fairway, but the standing water would literally cover half of the ball. So, we bagged the remaining holes and went to the clubhouse.

STRONG MENTORSHIP

Tom is a schematic and strategic football guru. Tom told me, as an offensive coordinator, from the press box he sees the field as a 3-dimensional chessboard. In my time of knowing Tom, not once have we ever had a conversation about the technical plays and schemes; nor specific plays that beat The Ohio State University's rival, "That Team Up North" (University of Michigan).

Tom's conversation was more focused on gratitude for the mentorship by Urban Meyer, The Ohio State University's Head Football Coach. Tom credits Coach Meyer and other head coaches he has worked under for teaching him the process of being a great leader, husband, coach, and father (not necessary in that order). Tom said his development as a football coach crystallized when he gained clarity on aligning the organizational growth of a team; managing the details of organizational setbacks; cultivating high expectations, and building a culture of competitive excellence. These are the real experiences that you can't find in an off the shelf leadership manual.

Organizational structures require

Disciplined People, Disciplined Thought, and Disciplined Action.

- Jim Collins, Good to Great

All of these coaching characteristics and experiences played out directly in The Ohio State University's 2014 Football season. All-American candidate and starting quarterback Braxton Miller was the front-runner for the 2014 Heisman trophy award. During the off-season, Miller was recovering from major shoulder surgery. The surgery and recovery was a success for the star player. A few weeks before the 2014 season opener Miller's reconstructed throwing shoulder blew out; this was a devastating season ending injury.

Buckeye Nation fans were in a full panic frenzy about the 2014 season, because teams are typically "dead in the water" when there is a dependence on a backup quarterback. To add to the hysteria, the second team quarterback was a redshirt freshman who was coming off a major high school knee injury, and he had no major college football experience. The team threw the freshman quarterback in the fire of top tier college football, and they stumbled miserably out of the gate for the first two games. The first game of the season, Ohio State was in a fight for their lives by squeaking out a win against a scrappy and less talented Navy team.

The following week, the Buckeyes experienced a stunning home opening loss to an average Virginia Tech University team. This bitter loss put the Ohio State fans in full three-alarm panic mode. At The Ohio State University there is a long standing tradition of ringing the campus victory bell after a football victory. It was an eerie feeling seeing 105,000 people exiting the stadium in total silence and disbelief. This loss was a major shock to the system and a deep setback at the start of a promising season. I believe Buckeye Nation chalked 2014 up as a lost season for a youth led team. Maybe the following season will be the year, the Buckeye fan base was ready to abandon the season and possibly concede a loss to rival University of Michigan. The fans were hoping that the team could win at least six games and maybe gain an invitation to play in a postseason Detroit Bowl game.

Tom's theoretical process seemed like a nice idea that didn't translate to application. Seeing Tom outside of the stadium, after the stunning loss, was a little awkward. When Tom came over to meet us after the press conference and team meeting, we weren't sure what to say. The Ohio State Football culture of disciplined people, thought and action was very clear by what happened next. With ice in his veins and a coldblooded tone, Tom said: "It was a rough day at the office, this week we'll have to continue working with the quarterbacks and our unit." Their team's culture had zero room for blame, shame, and excuses.

"I have to get my unit better and do my job."
-Coach Tom Herman

In The Ohio State University's football program, I suspect every coach, graduate assistant, player, trainer and front office staff had the same mentality and alignment of systemic self-improvement. Vertical alignment of the organization goals and mission was a critical component of organizational culture development by Head Coach Urban Meyer. Little does the average fan realize that fidelity and systemic alignment determine the levels of success achieved by elite teams.

Against all odds and enduring the hysterical discontent of local sports radio talk show hosts, the Buckeye football team's process of continuously developing the team's culture seemed to work. The Buckeyes went on a great winning streak for the remainder of the 2014 regular season. The team's process began to crystallize, and coaches kept investing emotionally in their players. The last game of the regular season was a showdown in what's known as "THE GAME." The Buckeyes geared up to battle in a no-holds-barred rival game against That Team Up North (University of Michigan).

"THE GAME" is the late November marquee event in college football. If Ohio State won, they would punch their ticket for a chance to play in the Big Ten Championship game the following week. The team was peaking at the right time, all phases of the team was aligned; like a V-12 American made muscle car, all cylinders were firing. The Buckeyes offense was a well-oiled machine led by a second team quarterback who was shattering Big Ten Conference football records. During "THE GAME," in the blink of moment the unthinkable happened; the star second team quarterback went down after a hit and he didn't get up. Inside the stadium 105,000 Buckeye fans were brought to a sobering hush.

I remember sitting in the stands and seeing the team doctor place a stabilizing air cast on the quarterback's ankle; and I knew it was broken. Injuries are part of the game, but this one made it seem like this team was "snake-bit" with bad luck. It was such a bad injury that the University of Michigan's quarterback ran onto the field to console his fierce Big Ten rival. The emergency squad assisted the quarterback off the field. For the 105,000 people in the stadium and the hundreds of thousands of Buckeye fans watching on TV, this was a collective punch in the gut. After the second quarterback suffered a season ending injury, fans were sure that a run at this improbable championship season surely was over.

In Columbus, Ohio it was DEFCON 1, knowing the third string Ohio State quarterback had to be ready to step into full action in less than five days. Most teams don't have a bench with a prepared third string quarterback. Naturally, the big question for Buckeye Nation was "How can the Buckeyes win the Big Ten Championship with under a week to prepare an unproven third string quarterback?" On a majority of teams the third team quarterback is usually some obscure kid holding a clipboard, chewing gum, and waving to his friends in the stands. Obviously, this guy is the third team quarterback for a reason.

So, after winning the "THE GAME" and the looming drama, we were standing outside of the football stadium by the car anxiously waiting for Tom to leave the locker room. After the game, the mood in Columbus was joyous because the Buckeyes just beat their rival and earned a prestigious ticket to the conference championship game. But, the Buckeye fans quickly came down from the high emotions and became gloom with the reality of a third string quarterback starting in the 2014 Big Ten Championship game, against a dominating Wisconsin team.

When Tom came out of the locker room, I timidly said "congrats my man!" As we stood by the car, I had no other way to say what everyone was thinking. In an uncomfortable, throat clearing, whisper I said, "Hey man, what's next with the frantic quarterback situation?" Astonishingly, not a hint of panic, he just looked at me with a big smile, leaned over and said: "he's ready... I have faith in '12-Gauge' Cardale Jones." I was totally perplexed and asked, "who is 12-Gauge?" With his big Cheshire grin Tom said, "the vertical passing game will be on point."

It was hard for me to believe it, at first. The next thing you know, after a week of preparation, the third team quarterback guided the Buckeyes to a massive victory in the 2014 Big Ten Championship. Come to find out the team calls him "12-Gauge Cardale Jones" because of the amazing strength of his arm. Jones was launching unbelievable passes that looked like the football was being shot out of a canon. After the Big Ten Championship game, the same third team quarterback guided the Ohio State Buckeyes to an improbable playoff win over the top-ranked Alabama University football team. Most impressively, the following week "12-Gauge" led the team to a win in the 2014 College Football National Championship against

Oregon University and their Heisman trophy award winning quarterback. This third string quarterback instantly became an institutional legend in the storied history of The Ohio State University.

The 2014 National Championship winning strategy was not about Ohio State's quarterbacks memorizing all of the technical X's and O's in the playbook. The winning of the football national championship occurred 24 months before the 2014 season. There was a clear process that each position coach and individual player owned. GRIT was one of the key ingredients in overcoming the challenges. But you have to understand, GRIT was not something established the week prior to the game or magically turned on the day of the game. Tom Herman emotionally invested in each one of the quarterbacks, his recruits, and their collective families. I know this is real because I witnessed it myself three months after the national championship game.

THE MOVE TO TEXAS

Before the end of the 2014 National Championship football season, Tom and I purchased concert tickets for our daughters. We figured this would be a fun outing in the spring. We promised the girls that we would take them to a concert in Cleveland, Ohio. Dads and daughters at a concert is a fun time had by all! However, the University of Houston unexpectedly offered Tom his first head-coaching job. He took the offer and was gone to Texas, while his family remained in Columbus for the next several months. I told Tom that I could take the girls to the concert, while he was recruiting and organizing his new football staff.

Once again, Tom reminded me that there are two distinct parts to this *"Process and Relationship"* equation. He wanted to totally invest as much quality time with his pre-teen daughter. A day before his first spring practice, as a newly minted head coach, Tom took the first flight from Houston to Cleveland. When we picked Tom up at Cleveland Hopkins International Airport, he looked physical and mental worn down. While Tom was loading his bags into the car, I asked him if he flew with the luggage under the plane because he was looking rough. Tom said he was averaging about three to five hours of sleep by pouring everything into his team. But, with the *"I don't want to disappoint my daughter smile,"* he was ready for a full day of fun at the Cleveland Air and Space Museum with the kids, before we went to dinner and the concert.

On our way to downtown Cleveland from the airport, Tom asked me to slow the car so that he can take a picture of the Cleveland skyline. I thought this was strange for a coach who will be living in a big skyline city like Houston. I just figured he wanted to take a picture to post on social media for Buckeye fans. Tom took the picture and sent a text message to his former third-team quarterback, Cleveland native, Cardale Jones. The message just said, "I'm in your town." I was overwhelmingly surprised by the authenticity of the brotherhood; the systemic process and authentic relationships are about as real as it gets. The equation to his blueprint was an unbreakable bond with his players. It hit me like a ton of bricks! I realized how and why the Buckeyes won the 2014 National Championship. The reality of it all was about the deep-rooted relationships between the players, coaches, and their families. Relationships were authentically nurtured and prized.

Months later, as a first-year head coach at the University of Houston, Tom and I were hanging out at the team hotel the Friday night before his first away game. With probably a million and one things racing through his mind, Tom paused for a moment in our conversation. A random Friday night college football game was on ESPN. Tom recognized the starting quarterback and mentioned that he remembers previously recruiting that kid. What's most amazing, Tom remembered every detail about the kid's family and the young man's personal life. This player was one of the hundreds of players Tom has interacted with over his twenty-year career. I'm not sure how many coaches would remember that much about a recruit that they never coached.

With the first full season behind him, I decided to visit Tom at the University of Houston during spring practice. I can clearly remember when he first started as head coach, how he stressed *culture over scheme.* What was unknown to observers regarding Tom, one of the most dynamic coaches in the country, was the manner in which he cherishes the family style atmosphere. College football is not a business to him; Tom always talks about the opportunity to add value to the lives of young men. This is a primary reason why he runs his team as an extension of his family.

The way University of Houston ran that spring practice, I'm sure it was typical of any other football team's practice. Yet, for me, one thing was different, the energy of the coaches and staff. The team seemed to crave the opportunity to train in chaos. Tupac was blaring on the stadium's speakers; players and coaches were head nodding to the beat, while maintaining focus on the task. Everything was up-tempo and everything was a competition to win something. At the end of practices the losing squad had to run extra sprints. The true game changer occurred when the coaches ran the extra sprints with the losing squad. The mentality was that we "ride or die" together, regardless of title or position.

During that same visit to the University of Houston, Tom helped me organize a free EdCamp conference for teachers in the greater Houston area. The University of Houston was one of the first elite universities in the nation to host such a collaborative event for K-12 educators. Tom wanted to be the direct point person to organize access to facilities. Tom even took time away from his busy schedule to meet with teachers and say a few words at the conference. One would think that coming off an unexpected Peach Bowl victory against Florida State University, the head coach at the University of Houston would not want to squander his time at a conference for teachers. It was exactly the opposite! Tom loved every moment of interacting with the teachers. What made me realize why he relished the moment was his heartfelt comments to the group of Texas teachers, administrators, and coaches:

"As coaches, we are educators at heart. When I was a kid growing up in a single-parent home, my coaches were my dads, and my teammates were my brothers...teachers are an extension of the family, and I love the innovative practices presented by this group."

THE DREAM CALLED: "HOOK'EM HORNS"

Tom's notoriety reaches beyond the wins on the field. As a pre-game ritual, the hugs and kisses on the cheeks of each player became a national story. Family and trust are the key ingredients great leaders apply to their organization. The hardest part about the coaching profession must be moving to a different job and no longer seeing the people you have formed relationships with on a daily basis. This was once again the case when Tom received an offer to become the next head football coach at the University of Texas, the flagship university of the state. Tom's emotions were running raw because he invested so much time and energy into each of his players at the University of Houston. But like any extended family, you may leave them, but you are never far away. This love for his players and their families was as genuine as it gets. The family style blueprint was modeled for the Houston players. Former Ohio State football players would visit Houston practices on a regular basis. This demonstrated to the Houston Football players that Coach Herman is serious about the extended relationship and he provides his former players with total access to his football team, regardless of where he might end up next.

Tom has weekly conversations with current Ohio State and University of Houston players that he recruited and coached. The conversations are hardly ever about football; they talk on a personal level, about real life events outside of football. Like I said before, for Tom Herman this is not a business; it's family. All former players have an understanding that they are part of Tom's extended family, the brotherhood. A high level of trust is a prerequisite of the genuine caring for the program and the fraternal order of the brotherhood. The true meaning of this brotherhood was evident on game day, in Houston's locker room for pregame against Florida State University. As I stood in utter amazement, I realized that not once did the players' conversation hinge on the game scheme and process. It was refreshing to witness the team's conversation was about togetherness; an emphasis on playing hard; and a clear focus on playing for your brothers. Not one player spoke about playing for future professional football league scouts, the team's culture frowned upon such talk.

Announced as the University of Texas head coach, Tom's number one priority was to have deep conversations with his young University of Houston team. Next, Tom wanted to visit with as many Texas high school coaches as possible, not to recruit, but to sustain an element of comfort. As emotional as it was for Tom to leave the University of Houston family, he found comfort in connecting with high school football coaches that he has known for over twenty years. Tom sees these great Texas high school coaches as father figures for young athletes, critical mentors, and he cherishes these authentic relationships. Most importantly, a relationship had been established. High school coaches trust Tom to do right by their high school athletes and their families.

Once again, this might sound like a level of spin or embellishment. There is truth to this "sacred brotherhood" that Tom has established; it's his DNA. In my latest trip to Texas, I had an opportunity to experience the aligned culture of the University of Texas' spring football practice. What stood out the most to me was seeing the raw emotion come out of Tom when I mentioned "the untold story of his culture." I found this story tucked away in an obscure picture on Tom's Instagram account. The casual picture was of Tom and his former Ohio State Football quarterback unit, during an off-season team building event. What's seldom talked about in that picture is the fact that all of Tom's Ohio State quarterbacks he recruited and coached are currently college graduates. I had to take a moment to think about the national college graduation statistics for African-American males. What's mind blowing is that Tom's entire Ohio State quarterback unit had a 100% African-American graduation rate. College football and a NFL career are not forever, but a college degree and the brotherhood last a lifetime.

When I mentioned this to Tom, his eyes started to mist up with pride. Tom's mission has always been to help his players mature as stronger men, fathers and become value-add leaders in their respective communities. This complex mission becomes simplified with the game of football. The players and parents entrusted Tom to do right by them, and he does. The trust of the brotherhood became more evident when Tom told me he received a signature game worn Buffalo Bills NFL jersey from his former quarterback, Cardale Jones. There was a note inserted with the jersey and it said, "this is my first and only game I played in, as a rookie; I wanted you to have my official game jersey."

As Tom told me the second half of story, he took a deep breath. Cardale Jones grew up in the urban core of Cleveland, Ohio. With Cardale graduating from The Ohio State University, he will be the first in his family to hold a college degree. Cardale personally contacted Coach Herman and asked (insisted) that Tom and his wife attend The Ohio State University's graduation ceremony, as his guests of honor. As Tom told me this story, I began to have an "allergy" attack and needed to get some tissues for my "itchy eyes." This authentic love runs deep and both ways. From an outsider's perspective, the grind appears to be about winning championships. The reality from the internal brotherhood perspective, the true grind is about building champions for life and the football championships will follow.

With the philosophy of building young men into champions for life, Tom has introduced the "4EverTexas" community-based learning series for players. The goal is to expose the players to various professionals and experts, in order to prepare players in their transition to manhood; this is a personal mission for Tom. Coming from a single parent home without a father, Tom knows from experience that it is hard to transition to manhood without mentors and positive encouragement. The building of a man requires a selfless mindset-the ability to sacrifice and do without in order for your family to have some. During spring practice, every player can hear Tom bark out to his University of Texas team, "It's NOT about you! It's about playing for your brothers; work harder!"

If you ever have an opportunity to talk with the University of Texas head football coach, Tom Herman; know that the topic will not be about championships; be prepared to hear how he welcomes *Champions to the GRIND!*

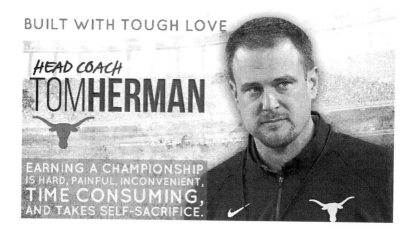

"WELCOME TO THE GRIND"

Nike Commercial: Rise and shine

It's 6:00 a.m. and your hand can't make it to the alarm clock before the voices in your head start telling you, *It's too early, too dark and too cold to get out of bed.* Aching muscles lie still in rebellion pretending not to hear your brain commanding them to move. A legion of voices is giving you permission to hit the snooze button and go back to dreamland.

But you didn't ask their opinion. The voice you chose to listen to is one of defiance. A voice that says there was a reason why you set that alarm in the first place. So sit up, put your feet on the floor and don't look back because we've got work to do. Welcome to the grind.

For what is each day, but a series of conflicts between the right way and the easy way. 10,000 streams span out like a river delta before you each one promising the path of least resistance. The thing is you're headed upstream. And when you make that choice, and you decide to turn your back on what's comfortable, safe, and what some would call common sense, well that's day one. From there it only gets tougher. So just make sure this is something you want because the easy way out will always be there ready to wash you away. All you have to do is pick up your feet. But you aren't going to are you? With each step comes the decision to take another. You are on your way now, but this is no time to dwell on how far you have come.

You are in a fight against an opponent you can't see, but oh you can feel them on your heels can't you, feel them breathing down your neck. You know who that is? That's you. Your fears, doubts, and insecurities lined up like a firing squad ready to shoot you out of the sky. But don't lose heart. While they aren't easily defeated, they are far from invincible. Remember this is the grind. The battle royale between you and your mind, your body and the devil on your shoulder who is telling you this is just a game, this is just a waste of time, your opponent is stronger than you.

Drown out the voice of uncertainty with the sound of your own heartbeat. Burn away your self-doubt with the fire underneath you. Remember what we are fighting for and never forget momentum is a cruel mistress. She can turn on the dime with the smallest mistake. She is always searching for the weak place in your armor; the one little thing you forgot to prepare for.

So as long as the devil is hiding the details, the question remains is that all you got? Are you sure? And when the answer is yes, and you have done all you can to prepare yourself for battle, then it's time to go forth and boldly face your enemy; the enemy within.

Only now you must take that fight into the open, into hostile territory. You are a lion in a field of lions all hunting the same elusive prey with a desperate starvation that says victory is the only thing that can keep you alive. So believe that voice that says you can run a little faster, you can run a little harder, and that to you the laws of physics are merely a suggestion.

"Nobody can judge effort, because effort is between you and you. Every day is a new day. And every moment is a new moment. So now you got to show them you are a different creature than you were five minutes ago."

So rise and shine. Let's Roll!

The GRIND is about systemic effort:
Improved processes lead to improved systems.

CHAPTER 1: JOB-EMBEDDED

A culture of greatness creates an expectation that everyone in the organization be committed to excellence. It requires leaders and managers to put the right people in the right positions where they are humble and hungry and willing to work harder than everyone else. A culture of greatness dictates that each person use their gifts and strengths to serve the purpose and mission of the organization. And it means that you don't just bring in the best people, but you also bring out the best in your people.

-Jon Gordon

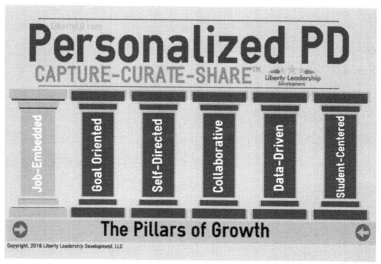

Contributing author, Thomas Tucker, PhD
Steven McGhee, MA

Job-Embedded process has an emphasis on the day-to-day act of learning and improving skills, thus, the art of the Grind! Making the direct connection between learning and doing is critical in any job-embedded approach, particularly as you develop your culture. The organizational culture is about what we actually do and accomplish. The priorities we set; the process we develop; and our strategic actions define our culture.

> *You cannot expect people to understand your grind.*
> *It is not theirs to make sense of if it's yours.*
> *Stay focused and fulfill your destiny.*

-by Tsepiso Makhubedu

DEVELOP YOUR CULTURE

The most critical aspect of any organization is the continuous development of a healthy culture and environment. Organizations often contact consultants for help with the implementation of various initiatives, evaluation, development of programs, analysis of efficiency, and fidelity of tasks. The critical factor that is most often needed is the performance management of the organization's culture. This chapter will examine how culture is manifested in community engagement, leadership styles, and strategically built into the day-to-day school schedule. The fostering of an organizational culture should not be the function of a response to an event. The culture is designed to enhance the priorities and values of the organization.

I want to be in an organization that treats me like family.

Too often, organizations are reluctant to acknowledge that culture is the bloodline and DNA of what they seek to accomplish; not just the development of a generic mission and vision statement, but the actual practices for success. Every organization has an established culture. Cultures can be strong and healthy, or weak and toxic. Regardless, there is a certain type of culture established within every organization. Culture serves as the neuroplasticity of the organization; the stabilizing bond during moments of chaos. Organizations have to choose if they want to invest in the development of a strong and healthy culture. It comes down to asking, "Do you want to maximize the performance of individuals and the organization, or become comfortable with mediocracy and the status quo?"

Within many organizations, people perceive themselves as being busy working on strategic initiatives. In reality, the people in the organization have settled into status quo; entrenched with complacency. So, how does an organization build a strong culture? This is not a new question, but it is often overlooked or simply ignored. It is important to note that by 2025, the Millennial generation will be 75% of the American workforce (Fry, 2015). Millennial workers want a positive work culture, regardless of the traditional financial incentives.

Organizations must recognize and accept that building a healthy culture is a continuous improvement effort that is both purposeful and strategic. Building culture should not be a "one and done" drive-by initiative. In fact, building a culture of continuous improvement comes down to the development of three critical aspects:

Consistency   Communication   Accountability

Consistency does not prescribe to a status quo or standardized experience for every person in the organization. Consistency means becoming an *innovative craftsman* of your skill. When consistency peaks, there is a strong emphasizes on improving and growing your professional skills, rather than working for bonuses or toward extrinsically driven metrics.

Consistency becomes a journey on a personalized pathway for growth and success within the organization. Each person works on self-identified levels of consistency, which orients toward meeting or exceeding both the organizational and personal growth goals.

Ineffective communication seems to be the breaking point for many organizations. Communication can come in many forms such as dynamic data, analytics, verbal cues, memos, and text. Most importantly, in a strong culture, *communication is strategic and purposeful.*

Communication is not a haphazard experience left up to individuals to generate. Great communicating organizations establish "voice and choice" as the drivers of vertically articulation and engagement at all levels. With voice and choice, individuals are empowered to provide descriptive feedback; therefore, the organization can develop strategic feedback loops as the formal method of communication. In great organizations, clear communication is empowering and valued. Through empowered communication, individuals develop ownership of their workflow; consequently, incubating a culture of innovation.

Accountability is often the third rail seldom to be explored. Too often, I've seen organizations blur the lines of accountability and compliance. These are two very distinct attributes, with the latter being a death grip anchor for those organizations seeking to move forward.

In great organizations, accountability is typically distributed vertically and horizontally. When accountability is at its peak, every person in the group internalizes their actions. Therefore, all members are accountable to themselves and each other. Most importantly, each member is accountable to people in the organization that they do not interact with on a daily basis.

Culture is the neuroplasticity of an organization; it bonds the unseen aspects of the individuals. A well-developed culture is paramount in the function of great organizations. These seem like simple tenants, but they require a level of commitment for systemic and vertical implementation. Growing and nurturing the culture is essential if professional growth is part of the organization's developmental goals. Once organizations develop a great culture, tremendous results will follow. Most importantly, everyone will see value in each other, regardless of official titles or years of service. In a great organization with a strong culture, people deliberately recognize each other's accomplishments. Give someone in your organization a high-five or "shout out!"

"Consistency, Communication and Accountability are keys to Effective Strategic Community Engagement."

Engaging community members in improving educational outcomes is critical. Both federal and local levels seem to agree that extensive government intervention in the "how to" community engagement process is not the answer for local implementation of educational reform policy initiatives. The challenge is the development of a comprehensive community engagement approach, in order to convert policies into best practices and results.

The first steps in community engagement are to identify who to involve and to provide clarity of tasks. Initially, two groups should be identified for engagement: grassroots and grasstops.

The grassroots are the local informal community leaders with prolific social capital in the community and a dynamic social network that can engage community members who feel left out of the decision-making process. These natural leaders are savvy with the amplification of information via technology or persuasive dialogue; most importantly, they can quickly mobilize community members.

The grasstops leaders are the local business and policy partners with critical access to legislative and monetary structures. The grasstops leaders can help advocate for and sustain the long-term goals of the local initiatives, even as local and federal leadership structures change. Engaging both grassroots and grasstops groups can create a robust driving force to amplify local efforts anytime and anyplace.

The initial phase of this robust community engagement process is featured by the U.S. Department of Education. The work at the local level by Detroit's Central Collegiate Academy high school is designed to build capacity and sustainability from a combination of community members and business partners. Implementing such a community initiative requires the development and cultivation of authentic relationships across all formal and informal groups.

In Detroit, like many other cities across the country, schools are the synergy of the local community. At Detroit's Central Collegiate Academy, the school made it a goal for students to engage their community by applying what is learned in school, to help solve local problems.

The school hosted a summative performance-based assessment gala with their various community engagement partners; students were able to showcase their efforts. The school combined both grasstops organizational leaders (General Motors USA, St. John-Providence Hospital, Detroit Parent Network, United Way, Sodexo USA, and Focus Hope) and grassroots leaders (students, parents and community advocates).

The high school students were provided with educational tours of these great community businesses. Students identified critical community needs and leveraged the corporate partnerships in order to help solve local issues. As a result, students were able to demonstrate how they applied what they learned in school, to enhance their greater Detroit community. Students provided performance-based demonstrations of their work with

Detroit homeless families, alternative and sustainable energy resources, and city family health services.

The community-based partnership produced a lasting effect in the community engagement process. St. John Hospital provided a partnership by providing a full health and wellness clinic inside the school. The community clinic was designed for students and families to have access to quality preventative health care screenings. The school and community identified family and human development, college access, and work force development, as critical community needs. Through the sponsorship of General Motors, the Detroit Parent Network, Focus Hope, United Way, and Sodexo the school was able to engage parents and families with the desired services. As demonstrated in this initiative, successful community engagement requires the input of all community voices, resources and skills.

The reason why the school was able to have such a success in their community engagement process was due to their block-by-block approach. The school identified every community membership group in each block of the school's attendance zone. The school recruited both grassroots and grasstops members into the school to develop a sustainable public-private partnership that is built to last.

Breaking News: Detroit Rising

Detroit's Central Collegiate Academy Has Become A Star in Urban School Reform

Increased graduation rate, ACT scores dramatically reverse recent trends

Columbus, Ohio -- (Nov. 20, 2014) Detroit's most historic, flagship high school has emerged as an inspiring success story in the city's struggle to reform its failing local schools. -- well above the national average for urban African-American students -- Central Collegiate Academy's Class of 2014 placed 88% of its students in postsecondary education, achieved a 78% graduation rate and raised average ACT composite scores by 1.7 points.

"We sat down as a school improvement and reinvention team, and put together a systemic plan to make improvements on the performance series as well as the ACT," said Central Collegiate Academy Executive Principal Steven McGhee. "On the performance series, our students moved up 1.5 to 2 grade levels on benchmark tests."

In addition to achieving numerical improvement on testing metrics, McGhee's team also implemented qualitative instructional improvements like one-on-one technology instruction for all students, internships in partnership with major area employers (General Motors), college tours, and job-embedded professional learning for teachers. Students also received assistance in completing scholarship applications and Fee Application for Federal Student Aid (FAFSA) forms, earning $1.4 million in academic scholarships.

The University of Chicago Urban Education Institute recently identified Central Collegiate Academy as the only U.S. Department of Education School Improvement Grant (SIG) high school in the city of Detroit, to earn a "Strong" (Organized for Improvement) rating.

"The University of Chicago research indicated that schools that measure 'strong' on three or more of the 5Essentials Survey of predictive change were ten times more likely to improve student learning. We are gratified at the results of their independent survey, and we are focused on continuing improvement to provide ambitious learning outcomes for our students," said Principal Steven McGhee.

Central Collegiate Academy was known until recently as Detroit Central High School, established as Detroit's first high school in 1858 and operating in its current location since 1926. Detroit Central was once the flagship high school in the city, producing accomplished graduates like billionaire philanthropist Eli Broad, U.S. Senator Carl Levin, Nobel Prize winner Melvin Calvin, NFL All-Pro Antonio Gates, "Inside The Actor's Studio" host James Lipton, and R&B singers Anita Baker, The Jones Girls, and Freda Payne.

Yet over the past several decades, the school suffered decline in academics along with the rest of the city. As Detroit's high school graduation rate declined to 38% citywide, third worst among the 50 largest U.S. cities, Central was ranked as one of the lowest performing high schools both in the state of Michigan and in the nation's 50 largest cities.

Since 2012, Central Collegiate Academy has been under the direction of the State of Michigan's Education Achievement Authority (EEA). Under a U.S. Department of Education's School Improvement Grant (SIG), Detroit Central High School was able to hire a McGhee as Executive Principal with the autonomy to replace staff and change the institutional culture.

Liberty Leadership Development, LLC, a comprehensive school improvement organization, was brought in as a lead partner to oversee strategic alignment of academic content and build internal leadership capacity through stakeholder engagement.

"Schools that focus on student learning often yield the highest academic results," says Randall G. Sampson, founder of Liberty Leadership Development. "We're extremely proud of our role in the dramatic success and turnaround achieved by Principal McGhee and his team."

Liberty Leadership Development was chosen to assist in leading a comprehensive approach focused on the full implementation of college and career-readiness content, rigorous instructional strategies and authentic student engagement practices.

FLIPPED LEADERSHIP STYLE

Educators are deeply engaged in the dialogue about the flipped class and how it works. It is great for teachers to be so engaged and ready to try different methods as they engage students in the learning process. Just as quickly as a teacher is burning with desire to learn a new practice, school leaders can become a wet blanket/barrier because their leadership style does not support teachers' need for innovation and change.

"Practices of the varied leadership styles are prerequisites for overseeing effective teaching and learning."

For teachers to gain the confidence in their innovative teaching and learning approach, the leadership team/administration needs to adopt the practice of Flipped Leadership. Flip leaders can be seen in most traditional leadership styles as long as the learning culture is job-embedded. Characteristics of transformational, participatory, and distributed leadership can be found in that of the flipped leader. Numerous studies have been conducted on principal and superintendent leadership and preparation for leadership; however, very little research has been conducted on the leadership practices of a flipped leader.

Preparing school personnel to be competent leaders and change facilitators can be accomplished through guided research leadership models such as Educational Leadership Constituent Council (ELCC) and the Interstate School Leaders Licensure Consortium (ISLLC) which were developed to influence school leadership preparation programs and professional development. However, until recently, little was known about the job-embedded flipped school leader model.

Flipped leadership is not designed to replace any particular leadership style. In fact, it is used to enhance any style. Peter DeWitt (2014) identified five job-embedded strategies that support the flipped model: (a) maximizes faculty meetings, (b) sets mindset before meetings, (c) parent engagement, (d) busy lives, and (e) focusing on learning.

Ohio's Dr. Thomas Tucker, National AASA Superintendent of The Year, takes the practice of Flipped Leadership a step further. Dr. Tucker works with his school district and schools throughout the nation, on developing the customized Flipped Leadership style. Empowering and developing leaders is a very personalized process because each community and school has unique needs for their specific culture. The goal is for leaders to add-value to their organization by leveraging their individual skills, in order to build exponential results. In his success, as a national leader of excellence, Dr. Thomas identifies the following systemic habits of highly effective flipped leaders:

- Engaging
- Well organized
- Capacity builder
- Empower others
- Relationship builder
- Champion of success
- Hard worker
- Visionary

Multiple Leadership Styles:

Failure is not an Option!

Leaders who lead a successful organization must firmly believe that success matters. Every day they enter their organization, they must commit to developing the people they work with on a daily basis and welcome themselves to the grind....

So how can school leaders who have been identified in a particular leadership style use the flipped habits and generate success?

Distributed Leader

The culture of distributed leadership has to be nurtured and grown over time, just as relationships. The work of the distributed leader takes place among the people in complex schools and other organization. Though developed and mostly used in education research, it can be applied to other domains. In a thriving school culture, multiple improvement initiatives occur simultaneously. A thriving learning ecosystem will require a balance of personalized and innovative tasks if the organization seeks to reach peak performance. The distributed leader will *build relationships* with those they serve in order to *empower others*.

Autocratic Leader

For the most part, teachers and leaders can agree that top-down leadership results are a short-lived autocratic experience. These leaders are focused on assessing the checklist of goals accomplished and compliance driven. In such a situation teachers often double-down with passive aggressive behavior; holding on until the top-down leader leaves. Therefore, a void in innovative practices becomes the norm of the learning ecosystem. Yet, they can still be hard workers.

The autocratic leaders seek to create a positive change in their school. Typically this person will recruit who they believe are strong teacher leaders in the building, thus *empowering others*. The leaders will assign the teachers to various tasks and committees, to accomplish school improvement goals or district-wide initiatives. Thus, they *engage others* and seek *hard workers* to complete the task. There is a high sense of external locus of control authorized by the principal, who is also micro-managing, the unauthentic innovation process. At a cursory level people in the school are working together, but have no authentic engagement, nor are they seeking to become creative innovators. The learning ecosystem stagnates and promotes practices of compliance.

Transformational Leader

The transformational leaders are *visionaries* and encourage learning to occur outside of the school and classrooms. Such dynamic leaders establish the conditions for teachers and students to try new methods and seek innovative learning, thus *building the capacity* of others while ensuring lasting *relationships*. Often time, the school's culture and innovation conditions do not reside within the expertise level of the principal or an individual. The ultimate goal is for teachers and students to amplify their strengths by actively *engaging* in real word experiences. Simply put, transformational leaders are *champions of success*, they *empower* at every level. They encourage learning tasks to be about the students and their world; building a strong sentiment for internal locus of control is at the heart of great leadership.

Intentionally Build An Organizational Schedule That Prioritize Relationships

Remarkably, a school's educational outcomes (standardized assessments, graduation rates or daily student attendance, etc.) are heavily predetermined before students start the school year. Schools can assure maximum student outcomes and achieve academic growth; a robust and flexible master schedule is the one essential element required to ensure proper planning for student learning.

A narrow focus on student learning and the school's mission.

Creating a master schedule should be a participatory process that includes teachers, custodial staff, grounds crew, cafeteria staff, central office, parents, students and administrative staff. Such an inclusive process allows everyone to have ownership of the vision and provide valued input for building a flexible master schedule. Schools that develop a culture of growth mindset, typically use the master schedule as a driver for their school's priorities. A flexible master schedule provides ample time for college and career readiness access, as defined by the school.

The school master schedule is seldom an issue of discussion or intense focus for policy makers or reform experts. Building a master schedule is a highly technical task, unique to one or two individuals in a school. Building a flexible master schedule requires an inclusive and participatory process for the learning community; in order to own the vision and deeply engage in the learning process.

Building a flexible master schedule is a three-phase process. The first phase- a clear systemic *understanding* of how all the pieces fit. It is important to ask those essential questions that serve as drivers of the process. The second phase- it is important to create a schedule that commits to future growth for students, in order to prepare them for college and career eadiness learning. The third phase- developing measurable goals focused on the academic development of *all* students.

Phase I   Systemic Understanding: Driver of the Process

Effective, flexible master scheduling evolves backward from the clear end goals to the people implementing the goals. The schedule is designed for schools to improve the long-term quality of learning for students. The schedule is flexible and provides autonomy for teachers and students, therefore ensuring sustainability.

Phase II   Commitment to the Future

- Examine current course offerings and assess if courses meet the rigorous college and career-ready criteria.

- Implementing research-based and best practice strategies for academic interventions (Response To Intervention – RTI).

- Create a course schedule that will provide teachers with an opportunity to teach a common cohort of students to enhance relationships and cross-curricular connections.

- Engage students, parents, and teachers in the vision of flexible scheduling to meet the needs of students.

- Develop a clear schedule of how we will maximize learning during the school day.

Phase III   Flexible Scheduling Goals

- Common planning time for teachers.
- Academic Interventions during the school day.

- Development of college and career-readiness mentors.

- Planned and purposeful data analysis of student progress and building new goals.

- Short cycle analysis of curriculum design and implementation (Unit and Lesson Plan Self-Assessment).

- Access to college and career- readiness experiences.

- Strategic planning and benchmarking progress.

- Gap analysis and strategic student support.

- Engaging students, teachers, and the community to bring relevance to the learning experience.

A school's master schedule should narrowly focus on the critical component of student learning and appropriate courses designed to meet the needs of a school's mission.

Scheduling Intervention Strategies

➢ **Intervention 6:** Special Education Program

➢ **Intervention 5:** Alternative Education / IAT Meeting

➢ **Intervention 4:** Study Center / Insight Class / Alternative Resource Center

➢ **Intervention 3:** A Case Review / Peer Tutor / Each One Reach One

> **Intervention 2:** Academic Referral Forms / Counselor Meet With The Student / Parent Phone Call

> **Intervention 1:** Initial Academic Watch List / Teachers Complete Academic Referral Form

Definitions

- *Academic Watch List.* A list of students who failed one or more academic classes the previous year

- *Academic Referral Form.* Used to track failing students

- *Each One Reach One.* Every staff member becomes a mentor to a struggling student

- *IAT Meeting.* Intervention Assistance Team Meeting

- *Case Review Meeting.* A review of any student who continues to fail despite previous intervention

- *Study Center.* After school study hall

- *Alternative Resource Center (ARC).* An alternative to study hall

- *Insight Classes.* Strategy classes for parents and students

Intervention 1:

Document an "Academic Referral Form" for any student(s) failing classes. At the beginning of the year, teachers are given an Academic Watch List to alert them to students within their classrooms who have a history of an academic problem. Students who fail one or more academic subjects (math, language arts, science, or social studies) are placed on an Academic Watch List that is distributed to teachers and administrators at the beginning of the school year. This serves as an alert that the students are "At-Risk".

Intervention 2:

On or about the time interim reports are to be distributed, teachers meet with any student who is failing and complete Step 1 of the Academic Referral Form with that student. Step 2 of the Academic Referral Form is completed for any student who continues to fail after the strategies outlined in Step 1 are implemented. The Academic Referral Form is given to the counselor after Step 2 has been completed.

If a student continues to fail, teachers will complete the Academic Referral Form and submit it to the guidance counselor. The guidance counselor meets with any student who has reached Step 2 on the intervention form and contacts parents. Teachers are given a list of those students who have reached Step 2 on the Academic Referral Form and are encouraged to "take one of them under their wing"(Academic Advisory). Peer Tutors and Study Centers may also be appropriate at this time.

Students who continue to fail may be assigned to the "Alternative Resource Center" rather than a study hall. Both parents and students are encouraged to attend an "Insight Class." If none of these interventions are successful, an IAT meeting is held to determine what other strategies and/or alternatives might be available.

The counselor meets with the student to discuss failure, reinforce strategies for success, and follow up with a phone call to parents.

A Case Review may also be held.

Intervention 3:

A Case Review may be held to determine what steps, if any, still need to be taken. In this intervention, staff reviews the histories of students who continue to fail. Students may be provided with a Peer Tutor, assigned to an AM or a PM Study Center, or linked with a staff member through Each One Reach One. This latter option encourages staff members to serve as mentors/advocates for low achieving students. A direct referral to the Intervention Assistance Team may be made at this time.

Intervention 4:

Teachers may refer students to a Study Center. This center is "subject" specific and staffed by a teacher who provides extra help to a small group of students before or after school.

Parents and students are encouraged to attend an Insight Class. Specific issues such as Study Skills, Appropriate School Behavior, Parent-Teacher-Student Communication, and the Importance of Attendance are addressed in a 1-hour session on Saturday morning.

The Alternative Resource Center (ARC) is assigned in place of Study Hall. The focus in ARC is concentrated on efforts to motivate students to accept responsibility for themselves, their academic achievement, and their ultimate success or failure by focusing on the completion of all academic work. No more than seven students are assigned to the ARC at any one time.

Intervention 5:

Alternative Education may be deemed appropriate for some students. Alternative Education includes such possibilities as Computer Instruction, Model Classes, and Independent Study. Staff may also meet to determine other alternatives to the normal education available to students.

The ARC is assigned in place of a large Study Hall setting. The focus in this Center is concentrated on efforts to motivate students to accept responsibility for themselves, their academic achievement, and their ultimate success or failure by focusing on the completion of all homework and other assignments. No more than seven students are assigned to the ARC at any one time.

Intervention 6:

The Intervention Assistance Team (IAT) meeting is convened to discuss any student who has been through the steps of the pyramid and continues to fail. This team will determine the need for a Multi-Factored Evaluation (MFE). An MFE could determine that Special Education Classes are required, and the student is assigned accordingly.

When deemed appropriate, a Multi-Factored Evaluation is conducted, and the student is assigned to the appropriate special education program if qualified.

CHAPTER 2: GOAL ORIENTED

All winning teams are goal oriented. Teams like these win consistently because everyone connected with them concentrates on specific objectives. They go about their business with blinders on; nothing will distract them from achieving their aims.

-Lou Holtz

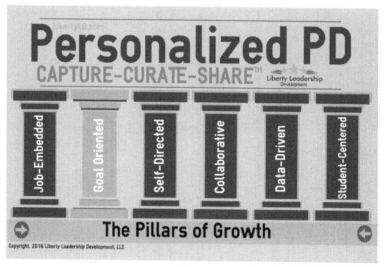

Contributing author, Sean Ross, PhD

Goal Oriented is an essential attribute of the Grind! Leaders must remain focused on the vision in order to achieve the ultimate goal of success. Aim for the moon; the goal is achievable. The most challenging aspect about this chapter is the ability to accomplish goals when there was no expectation for success. Success is achieved when the organization has a clear vision, matched with actionable goals.

We choose to go to the moon!

Meeting the challenge of education innovation; the boldest technology advancement made by man was accomplished through the challenge proposed.

President John F. Kennedy.

The Apollo 13 Mission of traveling to the moon demonstrated our human ability to overcome adversity with grit and adaptable technology. The education profession is in the middle of its "Apollo 13" challenge. Teachers and students are being challenged to engage with new technology that has never existed before, to maximize productivity for college and career-readiness. We are asking a vast majority of teachers and students, without formal educational technology training, to advance learning through the use of advanced technology. Teachers or students have never used the level of innovative educational technology available.

We have a failure to launch because both teachers and learners were groomed in a learning environment that rewards "tell me what to do" compliance and status quo. Our "Education Apollo 13" moment will need innovators, cage-busters, and disruptive leadership; strategically think different, to propel learning. Does the education profession have enough innovative juice to bend the arch of history?

An ad hoc educational technology scheme will perpetuate teachers' initiative fatigue, risk aversion and enhance frustration with the "flavor of the month" education reforms. Similar to meeting the Apollo 13 challenge of over four decades ago, I believe the education profession can meet our educational technology "Apollo 13" challenge.

The successful launching of educational transformation has to be highly strategic, goals focused and provide continuous training. It is critical to purposefully empower teachers, through the effective leadership. We want teachers to be the thought leaders and designers of the learning process. We want teacher to simply be....*effective teachers*.

EFFECTIVE TEACHING

The Gates Foundation Measure of Effective Teaching (MET)

In 2009, the Bill and Melinda Gates Foundation launched the Measure of Effective Teaching (MET) Project. The focus of the project was to find a balanced approach (classroom observations, student surveys, and student achievement gains) to measuring and predicting those specific effective teacher practices that have a positive impact on student learning outcomes.

With over 3000 teachers from seven geographically diverse U.S. public school districts volunteering to participate in the project, the results demonstrate a new day for the future of teaching and learning. I want to take a closer look at the MET Project by going back to its origins. The student survey component was started by the influence of teachers and practitioners several years ago, and those efforts laid the groundwork for the results we have today.

Back to the Future

The one aspect of the MET Project that I believe will help districts and schools gain critical insight into the learning process is through students' surveys and their classroom learning experiences. From 2002-2007 the staff at the Westerville Ohio school district, where I worked, used Ron Ferguson's methodical and robust Tripod Survey (MET Project Instrument) to gain keen insight into students' perceptions of school life. But, as the state of Ohio and the nation began to investigate the use of value-add learning measures, it was unclear to our staff what specific teaching and learning practices caused value-add to increase or decrease with their respective students.

In 2007, I called Ron Ferguson and asked him if we could couple students' three-year Math and English state standardized performance data with the three-years of Tripod students' perception survey data.

I thought maybe we could predict what it takes to increase value-add learning outcomes based on students' Tripod perception survey trend data. This perception analysis proved to unlock the great mystery for teachers and gave us the answers teachers were seeking. The teaching and learning process was crystallized for our teachers and students because our learning community could focus on those levers of change that yield the value-add results we sought.

With the student survey tool and value-added predictor, the landscape for teaching and learning will forever be changed. The game changer is that students' voices can directly impact their learning experience, coupled with teachers developing a stronger sense of efficacy and internal locus of control.

I remember at the start of the MET Project, a Gates Foundation representative was having lunch with me and asked why I thought the student survey value-add method could work for schools? My response was simple, "When our teachers reviewed their students' survey data and value-added analysis, they said 'we can do something, and we know exactly where to start.'" Our learning team's plan might seem simple or complicated to some, but it was the plan that our team created and owned. The key, we found, was to create a well-scaffolded plan that was feasible and can be implemented by the entire team (students, teachers, parents, and administration).

The question remains, "How will this MET Project help enhance or scale the future of learning?" The work accomplished by our teaching and learning community began to generate a new crop of cross-fertilized ideas and practice.

As we re-engineer the future of learning ecosystem, we will see learners creating rich opportunities; learners become self-advocates; the creation of local and national data systems to identify the conditions that yield high-quality learner outcomes; and schools (virtual/traditional) becoming national hubs of innovation and community resilience. The MET Project has cast a wide open net for which we can harvest the best teaching and learning experiences with equity and access for ALL students.

Yet, achieving any goal is least effective without a PLAN!

EFFECTIVE PLANS FOR EFFECTIVE TEACHING

Using the ACT predictor, Plan-Do-Study-Act (PDSA), and 21st Century Aligned Assessments are methods used by Liberty Leadership Development to support effective teaching that has helped schools move from *simply good to simply awesome!*

Creating plans for rigorous learning is necessary to support planning for effective teaching. The ACT Predictor is another tool used to initiate productive conversations between students and teachers; therefore, learning behaviors associated with the PLAN assessment gains can be predicted. The sample ACT Predictor (Appendix A) and the Honors/College Prep Course Enrollment (Appendix B) are examples of planning for recruitment for advance placement and post-secondary courses. Another effective planning tool used by teachers is the Plan-Do-Study-Act (PDSA). Additionally, the 21st Century Aligned Assessments called Identify-Develop-Practice is another method for effective planning for assessments.

ACT Predictor

The ACT Predictor does not predict the scores or range of scores students will produce. The ACT Predictor merely provides the learning community with a lens to students' academic performance on the PLAN ACT assessment. The PLAN assessment is an ACT predictor that provides students with a possible ACT scoring range. The ACT Predictor grid attempts to expand the academic story as it pertains to students' academic courses. It would be very helpful for teachers to analyze the range of possible ACT score as it pertains to the Honors courses that students are and are not taking. The data can be specific to individual teachers, per content area.

Such rich information can create deliberation for professional learning communities. Teachers and students can discuss what learning styles or instructional strategies enhanced students' scores on the PLAN assessment. Such dialogue can move instructional practices and learning styles to new heights by providing more depth to the learning process.

Plan-Do-Study-Act (PDSA)

Plan

Creating Plan for Rigorous Learning: Plan-Do-Study-Act (PDSA):

Our School Goals

- Increase academic achievement for all student subgroups.

- Provide a safe and positive learning environment.

DO

Specific areas of focus in the 20__-20__school year

- Implementation of a student-teacher advisory.
- The increase in AP course enrollment for ALL student populations.
- Decrease student suspension and/or expulsion rates.
- Increase the collaborative time for staff focus meetings.

STUDY

Documentation of progress towards goals

- Standardized assessment longitudinal data report card history (3-5 year trends).
- Short cycle standardized assessment results.
- Identification of learning gaps.
- Results from credit recovery and academic intervention teams.
- Access and monitor assessments in a comprehensive data warehouse.
- Incoming freshman performance data and support systems (Front end identification).
- Student quarterly progress reports.

ACT

What did we learn, how can we improve?

- State testing data (Identify the percentage of 11th/12th graders still need to pass 1 or more portions of the state assessment.)

- Implementation of daily proactive intervention.

- Collaborative learning environments can promote higher levels of student outcomes.

- Development of a rigorous core curriculum for *ALL* students.

21ST CENTURY ALIGNED ASSESSMENTS: IDENTIFY-DEVELOP-PRACTICE

The focus of Race To The Top-District applications is to increase students' educational outcomes as measured through summative assessment performance, decreasing achievement gaps by increasing attendance, graduation, and college enrollment rates. The path to such an ambitious initiative resides in the development of a 21st Century formative assessment process. A robust 21st Century formative assessment process is designed to provide immediate descriptive and contextualized feedback for both teachers and students during the learning process.

"The secret of the universe is 'task predicts performance.'"

-Richard F. Elmore, Educational Leadership, Harvard

Formative assessment occurs when teachers provide immediate descriptive feedback to students' learning tasks in ways that enable the students to demonstrate their learning in a meaningful manner, or when students can engage in a similar, self-reflective process. Such a personalized assessment approach can spur the college and career-readiness summative assessment outcomes most school districts aspire to accomplish.

Rigorous aligned assessment is a three-phase process.

- **Identify** the purpose of formative and summative assessments
- **Develop** the formative assessment classroom learning conditions
- **Practice** formative assessments daily (student tasks)

Identify:

Summative Assessment Is Focused On...

- Pre and post tests, end of unit test and quiz and chapter test
- State and national benchmark assessments—State

Assessments, ACT, SAT, PLAN, and PSAT

- Allocating grades
- What is learned or what students have not learned without re-teaching

- Teaching and teacher engagement
- Independent work/worksheets/multiple choice/true-false

Formative Assessment Is Focused On...

- Students asking and responding to questions
- Students interacting with each other during learning activities
- Direct and immediate descriptive feedback to learners
- Real-world problem solving embedded in the learning process
- How students learn and in progress re-teaching
- Short-term student learning goals and shared understanding, i.e., chunking the learning and unpacking the standards

Develop:

With 21st Century Formative Assessments for Classroom Learning Conditions, Students Will:

- Understand...
- Learn by...
- Discover...
- Explore, probe and problem-solve by...

- Connect with people and develop social skills by…

- Make personal connections to other students and their community by…

- Address issues and dilemmas by…

- Demonstrate creativity and originality by…

Practice:

21st Century Formative Assessment Student Engagement and Learning Strategies:

- Goal Setting

- Analogous Thinking

- Role Play

- Bell Ringing

- Point-Counterpoint

- In Your Words

- Card Sort

- Mind-Mapping

- Think-Pair-Share

- T-Chart

- Quick Write

- Text Annotation

CHAPTER 3: SELF-DIRECTED

"It always seems impossible until it's done."
-Nelson Mandela

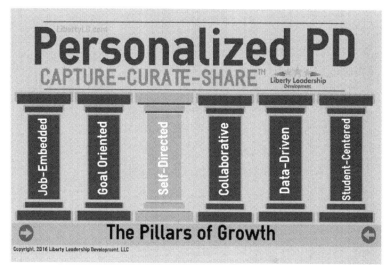

Contributing authors, Derek Oldfield
Daryl M. Woodard
Laura Cross

Self-Directed student-centered learning is the only way to truly understand the Grind! You have to understand learning from multiple perspectives in order to truly know that learning happens in numerous ways. Innovation in learning is amplified when the learners can explore their interests, become inquisitive learners, and prepare to solve real world problems.

We choose to see the light!

Rise by learning. Knowledge is never bought on counters or sold in any store, knowledge is the transferred Light from teacher to student...

-by Malika E. Nura

BLENDED AND STUDENT-CENTERED LEARNING

The mathematics teacher's perspective

Blended and student centered: that's how I would best describe the environment in my secondary math classroom. My professional learning transformation over the last four years was influenced by many digitally connected educators; mainly through the use of Twitter and social media. I can say with certainty that Twitter provided the exposure I needed to admit what used to occur in my room was poor practice.

Students in my class, five years ago, were subjected to very teacher centered instruction developed around a barrage of worksheets. I read Sal Khan's book "The One World Schoolhouse: Education Reimagined," around the same time I signed up for Twitter. Both of those experiences lead me to reconsider how I exposed my students to surface level, foundational depth of knowledge 1-type learning. When I realized I could eliminate the time spent checking answers to worksheets and writing grades with my red pen, my next step was to consider how I would replace that time. I acknowledged that a computer could assess student progress on problems that ask students to compute, calculate, simplify, or solve much quicker and more efficient than a human can.

It's necessary for students to perform those low level (Bloom's) verbs and I believe they do need consistent practice. My problem was 90% or more of my classroom time was spent measuring student progress against those types of problems. I never felt I had the time to engage my students in higher-order thinking like analysis, investigation, or prediction. I knew that level of engagement was required to strengthen the level of learning occurring in my class. I also did not have time for project based learning, outdoor experiences, blogging, or one-on-one conferencing.

Leveraging technology that allowed students to practice skills in an environment where they received immediate feedback; had access to resources for support, and we're a couple clicks away from rich data. The use of charts completely transformed the way I looked at learning. This allowed me to take steps towards providing students autonomy over their learning. It was also the time I started to reflect on my grading practices.

A fundamental theme in my classroom now is one size fits none. The steps I took above laid the groundwork for me to provide students choice over simple things like the number of problems they completed for practice. The students and I quickly learned that if a person could demonstrate proficiency in a specified learning target by practicing 15 problems in an environment that provided them constant feedback, then why should I require them to do 30 problems? This new awareness also forced me to consider why I was still demanding students learn according to my timeline. My assessments still rode on a conveyor belt and students had to complete those assessments according to my schedule.

Let's fast forward. Now, the buffet of opportunities that I provide students increase in quality. The vast choices students can make in my class have also increased. Students are firmly in the driver's seat now. I can provide students the menu, including self-assessment tools, and I invest time teaching them to monitor their individual progress compared to specific learning targets. So how does it all work? In the image below you'll see a chart I recently provided for my math lab students. Math lab is a remedial math class for incoming freshman at my high school.

Slope-Intercept Form

- I can identify the slope of a line on a graph.
- I can evaluate the slope of a line given two points.
- I can graph a line given it's an equation written in lope-intercept form.
- I can write the equation in slope-intercept form given a line on a graph.

Levels	Practice	Progress Checks (How am I doing)	Tests
1	• Graphing Points • Finding Slope • Finding Slope from Two Solutions • Slope Intuition	• Nearpod: Interpreting Slope and Y-Intercept	
2	• Graph from Slope-Intercept Equation • Slope-Intercept Equation from a Graph	• Self Assessment in Edulastic, sign in with Google account. Give three attempts.	
3	• Desmos: Your First Desmos Activity. If you do not complete it in a class period, just rejoin later. • Desmos: MarbleSlides Lines.		• Slope Intercept Form & Equations of Lines V1 • Slope-Intercept Form & Equations of Lines V2 • V3 TBD

That image comes straight from our learning management system. I create this page for students, and they have open access to it. The links take students to the outside resources that make up the buffet for those specific learning targets. I can break down the next few weeks in three phases.

1. Initially, there will be some moments of direct instruction, but most often that occurs with smaller groups of students.

2. After some initial exposure to the concept of slope or evaluating the steepness of a line, I may allow my students time to investigate further within one of the practice assignments.

3. Within the assignments, students receive constant feedback. I would spend most of my time on a knee bouncing from table-to-table offering support and advancing thinking with proper questioning.

I believe in putting the problem back on the students and this time is where I hone those questioning skills. At the end of the day, I take the opportunity to review some data from that class period. I typically find that a few students were able to demonstrate a measure of proficiency with that simple task of identifying the slope of a line. Most of the time those students were able to do so without my support. My presence at the tables during their work provides me with enough formative feedback to proceed the next day. In some cases, I may leverage those few students who did well by strategically seating them in positions where they may influence the learning of their peers. We have left the instructional phase and entered the practice phase. At this point, most students are practicing, but you'll notice the phases get a lot more fluid.

I may retreat to the instructional phase when a few students move on to a learning target that I have not yet provided any instruction. Once again, though, that most generally involves smaller groups of students. I find direct instruction is more effective in smaller groups. Disrupting the pace of learning may elicit fear and anxiety in some educators, but it liberates me to spend more quality time with students. Notice I said quality time. It's not that I'm getting more time, it's that I see a tremendous increase in quality time. It's also important to note the impact that it's having on students. Hope is the most important factor. Students have more confidence, motivation, and hope when they are aware of the destinations and can monitor their progress towards those targets.

The last phase is the assessment phase. I want to emphasize what students have completed in order to get to this point. Often I use Google Forms to provide my students with opportunities to reflect on their progress towards specific learning targets. I find that forcing students to engage in reflection is critical to developing metacognition and an awareness of their progress. If I weren't intentional about asking my students to reflect, it wouldn't happen naturally. Before incorporating this practice, my students would meander through the buffet of learning opportunities, take a test and receive poor results. During my conference with that student, he/she would express a measure of shock about their score. The student and I would retrieve the formative data that would reveal his/her practice efforts. Almost without fail, the data would reveal that the student had not demonstrated proficiency before attempting the test.

Occasionally this conference also provided me the opportunity to talk about the student's attendance, the distractions in class, or his/her work ethic. The goal of any student conference is to expose strengths and weaknesses, provide possible solutions, but also to promote autonomy. Autonomy is a critical component of cultivating learners. My grading and assessment practices mirror standards-based learning principles. Without covering that topic in depth, I incorporate a system of feedback alongside multiple opportunities to demonstrate learning. The feedback piece is critical. I never grade the process or the journey, only the destination. I often get this line from other colleagues, "if I don't grade it, they won't do it." That statement is true in a classroom absent of quality, descriptive feedback. Most often those students lack quality feedback, which will breed motivation.

The rate at which students acquire and demonstrate learning is much faster now. With the additional time, my students have been able to pursue blogging and video creation over the last two years. Those pieces are still relatively new, and I am always looking for ways to improve them. I intended to invest in blogging so my students could create and store artifacts that would represent their learning throughout the year. I have also started to allow my students to create learning materials for their classmates. Recently my students prepared materials to help their classmates prepare for the semester exam. Students chose to create Kahoot, Nearpod lessons, Padlet, and more traditional study guides. Those experiences revealed high levels of thinking, which I did not anticipate. For example, students had to unpack the essential learning targets and decide what they would identify as mastery. Whatever they decided, it was reflected upon through the level of questions and answers they provided in their study materials.

This blended learning image is one I created about four years ago, and it still guides my classroom today. Blended learning was the vehicle that propelled me towards a student-centered classroom and empowered me to provide a more rigorous buffet of learning opportunities for my students.

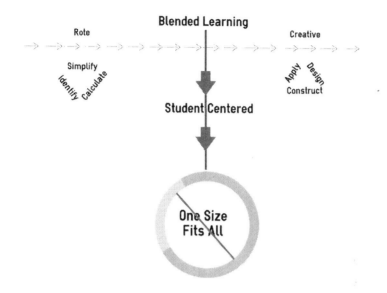

BLENDED LEARNING FOR QUALITY OUTCOMES

Title 1 funding is an allocation of federal funds to help improve the learning and academic achievement of disadvantaged students. The mission of Title 1 is to provide students in poverty with equitable access to quality learning assessments, well-trained teachers and rigorous instructional materials and pedagogy. The key transformational aspect of Title 1 is how schools and districts choose to use their funds. Title 1 schools can use the funding to engage students and parents, monitor academic progress and supplement instructional practices. To accomplish the mission of Title 1, schools can leverage Title 1 funds for the implementation of blended learning technology, training, and implementation.

Title 1 funds must be used to promote: High academic achievement for all children; A greater focus on teaching and learning; Flexibility to engage local initiatives; Improved communication among schools, parents, and communities.

Blended learning can be the critical driver for Title 1 schools seeking to implement innovative learning systems. A rigorous Blended Learning platform can enhance content, pedagogy and student engagement. As schools begin to use Title 1 funds to enhance learning through the use of technology, Blended Learning can become an essential lever used to propel a school's continuous improvement plan.

The key challenge for Title 1 schools is the ability to repurpose and leverage funds; this will help schools invest in a more efficient implementation of their continuous improvement plan.

Most states, districts, and schools (including Title 1 schools) attempt to have a systemic focus on educational innovation options such as Competency Based Learning, Project Based Learning, Community Based Learning and Parent Engagement. With these innovative learning approaches, Title 1 schools should be able to provide students with pathway options such as Online Early College Access, Job Certifications, STEM, Critical Thinking and 24/7 progress monitoring of learning.

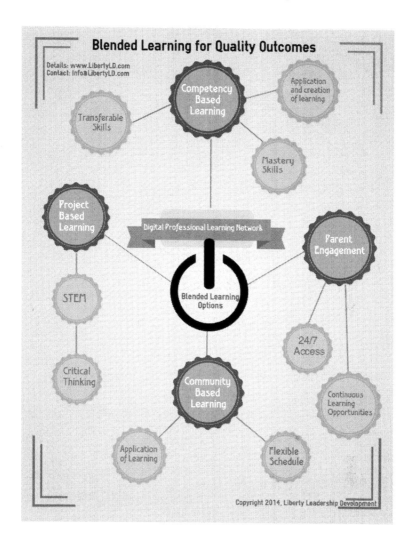

All of these learning pathway options can be leveraged efficiently with one essential platform. Blended Learning can provide students, teachers, and parents with a digital platform to:

1. Supplement the school's innovative learning pathways.

2. Monitoring students' academic growth.

3. Equip educators with more digital tools for differentiated instruction.

4. Engage students in academic content and workforce development.

Title 1 students, parents and teachers are not seeking a race to the bottom approach to learning. Students in poverty have the same hopes and dreams as their peers. Poverty should not be a prescribed destiny to failure; students in poverty want to be successful in their future endeavors.

APPLICATION OF KNOWLEDGE

The ingenuity of learning innovation

The U.S. continues to lag behind many industrialized nations as measured by the international summative assessment Programme for International Student Assessment (PISA). The question seems very simple to me. "How is this possible?" The solutions are complex and nebulous because learning practices do not align with the critical outcomes, required by the PISA. Creating a "show-me" type of learning environment, often referred to as performance-based assessment, creates a learning culture focused on knowing and doing inquiry-based learning. The ability to test and defend a proposition creates a vibrant level of debate and stimulates the levels of inquiry in the learning environment; thus, spurring ingenuity and innovation.

Tackling the PISA learning tasks, schools can infuse 21st Century Learning Skills as a remedy. 21st Century Learning Skills are compartmentalized into six performance-based student learning tasks that we call the 6-Pack. The 6-Pack is a research-based systemic approach that can be applied in the learning tasks of any instructional unit or lesson plan, as both formative and summative assessments.

The 6-Pack instructional design is not another "flavor of the month" stand-alone instructional strategy or theoretical framework. Utilizing the 6-Pack requires students to reconstruct learning by focusing on the synthesis, application and creating of information. Thus, the 6-Pack, a performance-based assessment process, can be strategically implemented by schools for students to increase rigor in their learning.

Empower learners to organize their learning into systemic structures.

The 6-Pack process is a system that empowers students to make a choice as to which assessment tool(s) they want to apply when demonstrating the application of learning. Students have a choice of which 6-Pack item(s) best illuminate and enhance their learning. Provided with a choice, the learners can use 6-Pack performance-based assessments to have ownership of their learning which leads to the articulation, comprehension, and application of the academic content.

An individual or groups of students can work on multiple 6-Pack tasks every day as a formative assessment component, leading toward the development of an authentic summative assessment such as the PISA. Students become more accountable for their learning, stay on task and are more engaged while utilizing these 6-Pack learning strategies. The 6-Pack strategies are an essential value-add for 21st Century learning communities seeking to propel the levels of ingenuity and innovation in learning.

TECHNOLOGY IN THE CLASSROOM

An urban middle school teacher's experience

When I was first encouraged by Dr. Sampson to use more technology at school, I was a little nervous. It wasn't because I am technology illiterate or anything; I am always looking to learn about the latest and greatest means of teaching and the tools to use while doing it. I was mostly nervous that I wouldn't be able to effectively teach content, and incorporate technology into my daily routine. I quickly learned that building technology into the daily routine was not difficult at all; actually, it was much easier. I also noticed that by using technology more often in my classroom, the behavior of my students improved drastically. I was able to talk, and students listened intently to what I had to say because they knew they would soon get to use the computer and do a task that was engaging, meaningful, content oriented and "Fun." I was thrilled.

What I had decided as a teacher was to do units in my class that taught basic skills and use the computers as much as possible, but to end each unit with a project that would showcase all of the skills learned in the unit. Our latest unit was an Autobiography Unit. Students did a formal Autobiography and typed it out like we had typically done in the past. Student engagement through the use of technology created more personalized 1:1 instructional time for the students. The project part was focused on students presenting their lives to me through the use of digital technology, using one of the several methods:

- A PowerPoint doing an AlphaBiography

- A slideshow that had them use each letter of the alphabet to describe who they are

- A GoAnimate in which they would create a cartoon character who talked about their life to another character

- A Glogster which would be an online digital collage to which they could upload pictures, videos and text

I was unsure of what to expect back from the students since I had never done anything like this before. The results I got were amazing! I had engaged, active learners in my classroom from the minute they walked in until the minute they walked out (which was 5 minutes late and I had to write passes because they wanted to finish).

With this type of project, my students were automatically using critical thinking skills because they had to figure out how to present their lives because I left it open-ended. By the second week of a three-week project, students were doing cartoons, Glogster and PowerPoint that were far more superior than the examples that I had given them. They began teaching me how to do some of the cool things that they had learned! It was a truly rewarding experience as a teacher.

To end the unit, we did a Gallery Walk in which we put all of the desks in a circle and students opened their projects up on one of the computers in the room. Students went desk-to-desk viewing others projects and leaving positive comments on sticky notes on the desk with the project.

Here are a few student responses to the project:

"I loved the Autobiography Project. We were able to do different tasks instead of just pencil paper work or a poster. I really liked that we were able to be creative with it and had multiple choices to do our projects instead of one choice like I said before: just paper and pencil. It was fun. I would love to do more projects like that." ~Lanice

"I loved working on GoAnimate and figuring out how to do a video and make it about my life. I loved creating the stories of my life through the stick figure people. I kept wanting to learn more and more about how to do the videos, so I played with it all night long at home. I spent two hours one night trying to get ponytails on all my girl characters. It was the most fun project I have ever done in school." ~Deztani

IT CAN BE DONE!

Accomplishing The Impossible In Only One Year

Public, Private and Public Charter Schools have been trying to figure out how to meet the student learning expectations as quickly as possible. There are demands and expectations that school systems can and should help ALL students meet and exceed the learning expectations. Too often, our educational system does not meet that expectation for many of our learners.

With the simple Liberty Leadership approach, schools are maximizing learning and can exceed expectations in one to three years. Yes, a clear process and commitment can systemically do that.

Wilson Preparatory Academy (WPA) is a new Title I Rural Public Charter School located in Wilson, NC. This K-12 Blended Learning school opened in Fall of 2014 and was mandated to administer the North Carolina End of Grade 3–8 Reading and Math Assessments in Spring of 2015. When WPA opened, the school had limited academic performance data of their new students, limited time to develop processes and no textbooks for instruction. Yes, NO TEXTBOOKS!!!

Every student was issued a Chromebook as the 1:1 Blended Learning instructional tool and used an adapted version of Project Based Learning as the student engagement framework.

As a result, WPA saw tremendous results on their North Carolina End Of Grade (EOG) 3–8 state reading assessment. In a short few months after starting the 2015-16 school year, the results were in; WPA met their academic achievement and value-add growth targets. WPA outperformed many of the established schools from the Eastern NC Region; Mecklenburg County (Charlotte, NC) Region; and Wake County (Raleigh, NC) Region. Most notably, in 2016 WPA outperformed the nationally acclaimed NC KIPP schools model.

WILSON PREPARATORY ACADEMY

* EVAAS GROWTH 15 TIMES THE STATE OF
NORTH CAROLINA'S AVERAGE
* TOP 20% K-8 READING PERFORMANCE IN NORTH CAROLINA
* TOP 15% SCIENCE PERFORMANCE IN NORTH CAROLINA
* 100% ON TRACK GRADUATION RATE
* +17% ACHIEVEMENT GROWTH
* +65% EVAAS GROWTH

ELITE LEARNING PERFORMANCE

In working with WPA staff, we DID NOT focus on out-performing other districts or schools. We made the process simple; we helped teachers foster a growth mindset. Teachers were able to concentrate on improving their craft and personalizing the learning experience for each student. *The school nurtured a growth mindset CULTURE of learning by being open to innovation and change.* Teachers and students were highly coachable in developing their culture. To establish the learning expectation, teachers did not accept poverty or previous learning experiences as liabilities for students' learning success.

Make no mistake, the teachers and students worked very hard. Common language, aligned professional development, and building a distributive leadership CULTURE are all of the critical ingredients required for success.

CHAPTER 4: COLLABORATIVE

"America still has the right stuff to thrive. We still have the most creative, diverse, innovative culture and open society - in a world where the ability to imagine and generate new ideas with speed and to implement them through global collaboration is the most important competitive advantage."

-Thomas Friedman

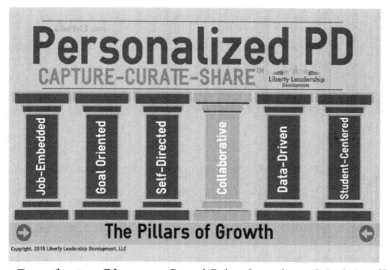

Contributing Olentangy Local Schools authors, Mark Raiff

Jason Bates

Zach Peterson

Scott Cunningham

Collaboration is how you engaged in the Grind!

The **Collaborative** process is essential for leveraging strengths and weakness in order to work together with a common purpose. Teachers, Principals, Community members, and the Superintendent demonstrates collaborative alignment of a school district's mission.

We choose to communicate!

Talent wins games, but teamwork and intelligence wins championships.

-by Michael Jordan

TOP PERFORMING DISTRICT

The Hedgehog: Core of Greatness

The "Good to Great" book by Jim Collins is a staple resource when organizations seek to improve their brand or model. Ohio's Olentangy Local School District serves over 18,000 students and is a national top 1% GREAT school district, as measured by The Washington Post and U.S. News & World. In 2015, all three of Olentangy Local School District high schools ranked in Ohio's top ten elite high schools category. To the average person outside of the school district, the question is "what is it that they are doing?" Surprisingly, this is not a question that drives the culture of the school district.

Jim Collins four stages organizations:

- Disciplined People

- Disciplined Thought

- Disciplined Action

- Build Greatness To Last

What makes Olentangy Local Schools a great organization is their remarkable ability to master stage two; maintaining disciplined thought. Typically people would misinterpret this concept to be a "like-minded drone" syndrome with no deviance for originality. Their level of disciplined thought is the opposite. The Olentangy Local School District's leadership team and teachers appear to strongly practice a discipline of innovative behavior, coupled with the "Hedgehog concept." So, Olentangy Schools rely on strengthening their values and mission. With a strong core, the district infuses innovation from the students' desks to the superintendent's door. Olentangy Local School's Superintendent, Mark Raiff, states "our schools have a simple strategic concept that we pursue with relentless effort," by always asking the following Good To Great (Collins, 2001) questions:

- What can we be the best in the world at?

- What are we deeply passionate about?

- What best drives our resource engine?

"Teachers have the autonomy to create an individualized professional growth experience."-Mark Raiff, Superintendent, Olentangy Local School District

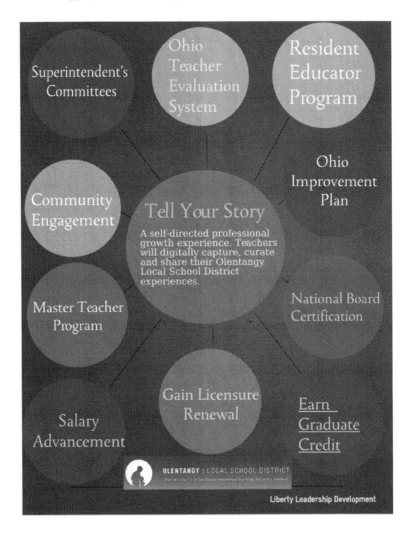

With this culture of greatness, the school district is providing teachers with the opportunity to capture-curate-share their

unique perspective of the school district's mission in action. Teachers have the opportunity to digitally capture what they are good at, passionate about, and how they apply the resource to meet their goals.

The school district invested in their teachers by offering "Personalized Professional Development (PPD): Tell Your Story" as a professional development course for graduate credit.

With this personalized professional development experience, individual teachers will be able to digitally capture and portfolio the specific classroom practices that work best for student learning. In a Hedgehog culture, Personalized PD is not another thing to do or a checklist "fad of the month" program.

Educators will have the opportunity to efficiently consolidate various state and district initiatives into a streamlined one-step approach, to build upon what they do best. Teachers will be able to use their portfolio evidence for National Board Certification, teacher evaluation evidence, Resident Educator Program, continuous improvement process, and community engagement.

Additionally, upon completing their Personalized PD of self-directed professional learning, teachers will earn graduate credit toward *licensure renewal* and *salary advancement*.

"Tell Your Story" is helping the Olentangy Local School District gain clarity about what practices they are good at and how to continue to build upon the innovation.

If your district or school seeks to know what they are good at, simply ask the passionate practitioners *"what are we doing well?"* Most importantly, offer the opportunity for educators to digitally capture their great teaching and learning moments.

"Building a K-12 systemic improvement culture requires empowering teachers. Our district recognizes the fact that teachers should have the autonomy to lead their professional growth."

-Jack Fette, OLSD
Executive Director of Curriculum and Instruction.

A Top Performing School: Hedgehog concept translated to practice

Learning in a PLC: Student by student, target by target

Collaborative teams in Professional Learning Community (PLC) schools use the four critical questions of learning to drive their collective inquiry and action research. These questions are fundamental to the PLC process:

1. What do we want students to learn? **(Essential Standards)**

2. How will we know if they have learned? **(Team-developed common assessments)**

3. What will we do if they don't learn? **(Systematic interventions)**

4. What will we do if they already know it? **(Extended learning)**

When considering critical question #1, I'm not sure the first time that I heard or read the statement "student by student, standard by standard" from a great mentor and Solution Tree icon Mike Mattos. But I do know that this statement has been transformational for my school and many of the schools with whom I work.

At Olentangy Orange Middle School we use the phrase "student by student, learning target by learning target." When we were developing a guaranteed and viable curriculum the educators involved decided to use the term "learning targets" instead of "standards."

Once educators truly understand what this statement means and how to use it to identify student's strengths and weaknesses to differentiate instruction truly; educators will see incredibly high levels of learning for all students and they address each of the four critical questions for every unit of instruction.

I want to share a few specific strategies that our teachers use to truly make sure that all students are learning at high levels, by not only knowing the phrase but also living the phrase "student by student, target by target."

Our staff uses question number 2 (**results from team-developed common assessments**), to truly answer questions 3 and 4 around **interventions** and **extending learning.**

1. We are very "tight" that our teacher teams instruct "student by student, target by target," but we are "loose" on how they do it.

We always encourage individual teachers to be creative in how they instruct and assess learning in their classrooms. Our teachers are continually looking for ways to improve their instruction to meet the needs of all students. As individual teachers test out new strategies in their classrooms, they can share insights with the other members of their collaborative teams.

2. We are "tight" that all of our team developed common assessments are aligned to learning targets, but "loose" on how teams indicate the targets on their assessments.

   Some teams put the learning target being assessed above the actual question, while others code the learning target beside each question. The teams who code the learning target give a sheet with all the targets and codes to the students, so they also know the specific learning targets being assessed.

3. We are "tight" that all students will be flex-grouped based on whether or not they achieve mastery of the learning targets, but "loose" on how the teachers flex group.

   Flex-grouping has become a buzz word, and when I've pushed people over the years to explain how they flex group, I often hear the same story over and over. In traditional schools, teachers give a baseline reading assessment and group students by their score on that single reading assessment. These ability groups can remain in the same class all year long, sometimes even with the same teacher resulting in high, medium and low groups, or tracking. This bad practice is frustrating because students are being ranked and sorted by a single test score.

4. We have taken a different approach to flex grouping at Orange Middle School, and we do it differently depending on the subject and the team. Below are a few examples.

Our 8th-grade social studies teachers align every question on each assessment to a specific learning target. Students then work in stations or groups across the social studies classrooms to relearn the targets they missed or do an extension activity if they achieved mastery of all targets.

Our 6th-grade science teachers assess students based on learning targets throughout a particular time span such as a week and then have an extension lab at the end for all of the students who have learned the intended targets. Any student who is missing targets during the week works on the targets in stations or groups, and as they learn the targets, they are then expected to complete the extended learning lab during an academic assist time, which is built into the schedule.

Our math department uses pre-assessments of the necessary prerequisite skills to flex group students to different teachers, before teaching the new unit. Based on the pre-assessment results, students either receive more support to learn the prerequisites or to apply the prerequisites in extended learning activities. Every student who does not demonstrate mastery of individual skills goes with one teacher, students who miss other targets go with a different teacher, and students who meet all targets go with another teacher for extensions. The teachers decide ahead of time; who will be in charge of the relearning opportunities for each target based on their strengths in teaching those targets?

Grouping the students based on mastery of learning targets instead of a single test score stops the high, medium, and low grouping of kids because they are all working on areas of specific needs based on progress towards mastering specific learning targets, not scores.

This method of meeting all kids' needs based on targets is transformational because students start to take ownership of their learning when they know their specific areas of strengths and weaknesses, and are expected to improve or extend their knowledge.

Before engaging in the PLC process, we had a culture in our school of "chasing the A," and as soon as a student would get a 90%, they would say, "well I got the A, so I don't have to do any more work." However when we truly live the phrase "Student by student, target by target" we no longer have to chase the "A" we can focus on high levels of learning for all, because we know specifically what kids know or don't know. We will no longer settle for learning 90% of the intended targets, or for most students learning most targets. Each student will learn all of the essential targets, and as professional educators, it is our responsibility to make sure that this happens for all of our students.

BUILDING PERSONALIZED LEARNING

What is holding you back?

From my first day in the teaching profession, student test scores dominated discussions and guided professional development. In Ohio, I began my career with the proficiency tests, and then the Ohio Graduation Tests (OGTs) came into play, and now we are moving into the Next Generation Assessments. Each time I would sit down and look at my students' data there were only a few students who surprised me with their results from the last year's assessments. Early in my career pride would lead me to the conclusion "you can lead a horse to water, but you can't make it drink." Of course in collaboration, I would look for better ways to present a lesson or track students' learning, but I nearly always found myself teaching to three distinct groups: the lower, middle and high. Regardless if I was teaching an inclusion, regular or honors class, I would predominantly revert to planning for these three tiers of student performers. My students' achievement scores were above average; I knew my students were learning at high levels, and our school and district were always in the top in the state and nation. So why would I change anything? Why fix something that is not broken?

My last two years in the classroom I began to notice that while something was not broken maybe it could be improved. While my approaches worked for the majority of my students, not all students learned in the traditional lecture-based, desk and row classroom. Perhaps my class, school, and district were one of the best in a system that is good, but could still be great. Why was I looking at teaching to different groups of students? My experience and common sense told me that each student was unique and each has different needs. Why was I not looking at finding a way of delivering instruction that allowed me to meet the needs of each student individually?

I started using much more self-assessment in the classroom.

From experience, I knew students performed better when they took ownership in their learning and could identify specifically what they knew and did not know. I could then target these gaps and more efficiently ensure each student was learning the material. I quickly noticed my accelerated students were moving more quickly through the material so I provided extension activities or encouraged them to explore concepts within topics at a deeper level. I also was provided more time to work individually with students who struggled with the material. Lastly, I quickly noticed that this was hard…really hard, and took A LOT of time. Although I did not realize it at the time, I was dipping my toe in the personalized learning pool. However, I had no idea how to most effectively and efficiently implement these approaches.

That winter I was offered a position as a teacher on special assignment, which turned into a full-time assistant principal position the following year. Implementing personalized learning was going to look much different. However, I was excited and energized to work with teachers in this area. My first year was a complete whirl-wind learning all the things one needed to know for the role as an assistant principal which you are not taught in your Master's program (a MUCH bigger chunk of information than I thought I would have to learn). As a result, I did not have much time to dive into personalized learning with the teachers in my building. The summer after my first full year as an assistant principal I attended a blended learning conference, and everything seemed to click. Finally, I thought, this was a way to better personalize learning! I could not wait to take my learning back to the building and share it with anyone who would listen!

At the beginning of the following year, I was eager and excited to slowly begin pushing the envelope and introducing pieces of personalized learning to the teachers with whom I worked. To my surprise, the new ideas were met with skepticism and uncertainty from many. I have to admit I felt deflated at first. But it was an opportunity to reflect and realize I was exactly where they were a few years ago. These teachers had some of the highest scores in the district, state and nation. Why would they want to change something that was not broken? How would they be able to personalize learning using blended learning approaches when not all students had access to technology every day? Where would they find the time to complete all this work?

I knew I did not have the answers to all of these questions. But I was eager to find teachers who were willing to take risks and challenge the status quo. Maybe this was how we take good or great teaching practices and make them even better. I used blended learning as the backbone to begin discussions centered on personalized learning approaches. However, I realize now that we should drop the word blended as the primary focus is on learning. I also realize that I may have scared some teachers off using the term blended learning, as some were less comfortable with the technology component and erroneously thought this simply meant flipping the classroom. Regardless, many teachers during evaluation season were open to learning more about personalizing student learning, but wanted additional resources and to see examples of what it looked like in practice and how they could begin infusing parts of this into their classroom.

Here are a few tips I gave them from my experiences in the classroom and observing other teachers in my new role:

1. **Start small**- Start with just one unit, part of a unit or even a lesson. Be sure not to overwhelm yourself or the students. Ask and listen to their ideas and feedback.

2. **Find a buddy**- While it may be better to find someone who teaches the same course(s) that you do to share the workload and materials, anyone who is

willing to try these approaches will be a great resource to share/bounce ideas off one another.

3. **Gather resources**- focus on instructional delivery and assessment. I shared resources provided by other teachers and admin to give them some ideas of ways to deliver instruction diffidently (SchoolTube, Schoology, articles I found on Twitter, Khan Academy to name just a few). I encouraged them to consider recording certain parts of their lesson – preferably the introductory parts in which most students do not struggle. This would allow them time to focus on students who were struggling with prior material, or allow them to work with students who were accelerated beyond their peers.

4. **Use the resources that work best in your classroom.** Not everything that works in one teacher's classroom will work in another. However, gaining a bank of resources will all allow you to personalize student learning even more. Using a platform for formative assessments that require students to demonstrate their learning before moving on will truly allow you to personalize learning and allow students to progress at their own rate. While it may look messy at times, as not all students will be doing the same thing at the same time, this is where some of the best learning can occur.

5. **Not every approach needs to be driven by technology.** There are times when direct-instruction

may still the best approach for the class, and video lessons are not quite as effective. This is ok and part of the learning curve. Determine which parts of the lesson/units can be pre-assessed to continue to the next topic, flipped, re-taught, small grouped, extended when mastered, assessed in alternative ways, etc. Find what works best for the students in the classroom, not necessarily what works best for the teacher in the classroom.

6. **Give students additional resources, if they do not understand the material.** Classroom learning opportunities should be a buffet and we should re-stock it with what students want and need to maximize their learning. When teaching AP Calc BC I often had students who would find videos on YouTube to re-explain the information or explain the concept slightly different than I had. Perhaps they just needed to hear it repeated 2, 3 or 4 times before it clicked for them. Nine out of ten times, THAT IS OK! And the information they are learning is correct; perhaps it was just explained slightly different than my explanation. My goal is that students are learning the material, not that I must be the only one teaching it to them. I want students to use their resources, just like they will have to in life. I had to use YouTube tutorial videos in an attempt change my garbage disposal.

7. **Take a risk – Make the jump!** Use different learning approaches/models, have a backup plan in place and do not get discouraged if it does not work perfectly the first, second or third time. This will allow teachers to reach the needs of more students yet leave them prepared in case the lesson is a flop. All great teachers have experienced this in some capacity. Just as students best learn through their mistakes, so do teachers. Learn what works and does not work, but do not get discouraged if the plan does not go exactly as you had hoped. Meet resistance with positivity from all stakeholders.

8. **Share your knowledge.** Let me and others come into your class to learn and experience the journey with you. Not everything will work the first time and it may not always be pretty. That is ok. I am not looking for a "gotcha" moment to use on evaluations. Let your buddy come in and get ideas and provide you feedback. Return the favor and observe others' classrooms to continue to refine the classroom experience for all.

I am always eager to learn and gain more resources to share with teachers to improve their craft and ultimately increase student learning. Therefore, I welcome anyone to share any resources that I can also pass along to teachers as it pertains to personalized learning. I sincerely believe students learn differently than I did; yet many classrooms look identical to my elementary, middle and high school classrooms. I charge all educators to challenge the status quo and transform classrooms to meet student needs. Change not only how we are delivering instruction but also what your classroom looks like! I truly believe this can help shift the focus to learning, curiosity, exploration, and authentic learning opportunities as it also reduces the focus on points and letter grades in classrooms. Just because what we are doing is good and sometimes great, it does not mean that it cannot always be improved. Is that not a part of why each of us went into education?

The Olentangy Classroom

Aligned Action

The first days of school I discussed the importance of cultivating a strong classroom culture. With a relational foundation on the ground, I now have the opportunity to share "WHY" my class is relevant, necessary, and beneficial. Without the precursor of "WHY," the day-to-day "WHAT" (curriculum, units, lessons, activities) becomes monotonous and obsolete.

As a lead-learner Spanish teacher my mission has two parts:

1. Facilitate a hunger for learning

2. Provide opportunities where students learn to satiate their hunger. (Note: Buy-in is the enemy of ownership. We want students to OWN their learning, not buy-in to what you're telling them to do…)

The Week of "WHY?" Goals and Rationale:

- **Validate the value of Second Language Acquisition.** Second Language Acquisition (SLA) is important because knowledge is power. While I could write a book on the importance of SLA, I'll sum up my favorite rationale like this: SLA does not drive, but enhance our career paths. From an employer's perspective: when an applicant demonstrates the ability to speak another language they establish value to my company. My hope is for students to share their career interests and dream what it might look like to pursue a field they are passionate about equipped with another language.

- **Introduce students to the educational value of specific YouTube channels.** I am learning that as technology evolves and ultimately changes the landscape of education; I must follow suit to provide a meaningful experience. This year I have committed to interlacing specific relevant (and FREE) technology/software within the curriculum.

- The technological focus for this unit (The Week of "WHY?") is YouTube. (Units will include interfaces such as Twitter, Voxer, Various Blogs, Pinterest, Flipboard, Typorama, Canva, etc.)

- **Facilitate discussion boards in the spirit of #EdChat collaboration.** Our school uses Schoology. This week my students did not take notes or fill out worksheets while we watched an educational YouTube clip. Instead, I facilitated interactive discussions in real-time on a Schoology discussion board.

THE EXPONENTIAL RETURN

The #EdChat format is a classroom teacher's dream. As lead-learners we need to create space for our students to learn and get out of the way.

Participation-Have you ever asked a question to a group of people and been disappointed you couldn't hear everyone's response? The discussion board is inviting and encouraging to every student. It replaces the anxiety towards public speaking with a manageable burden to contribute to the team effort.

Collaborative Documentation-The EdChat/Discussion replaces individual notes and mind-numbing worksheets. When students complete worksheets they are ALONE; they do not have anyone to keep them accountable or challenge them. The EdChat/Discussion board acts as a shared stream of intelligence where students are motivated to contribute to their team of classmates.

Student Engagement- Students engage by using devices. Students are not addicted to their phones; they are addicted to being connected. (Spoiler alert: they're no different than us in that regard. We're human. Humans are relational creatures who desire and need to be connected.) Throughout the week I have noticed that students are motivated to sign-in and get involved because I am using an interface that is relevant. When they sign-in, they are connected to their classmates, connected to the curriculum, and connected to the learning process.

Differentiation- As a participant in the discussion, I frequently post, reply, like, and challenge student posts. students are given a single task when posting or replying: "Invite further conversation." Posts that do not enhance the collaboration, (ex: Awesome! That's great!), are encouraging but do not enhance our team's body of work. Students who are advanced in their thinking, typically post early and often. I can readily differentiate instruction by challenging their thought process, debating the other side of an argument, or asking questions to continue their train of thought. Students who require extended time or clarification can take their time and post at their pace. Because of our culture, I often get beat to the punch when attempting to differentiate. For example, if a student's post requires clarity, other students are quick to provide information and support their peer. Compliance is a hot topic in education. Educators are continually looking for ways to help students take ownership in the learning process. Throughout this activity, my Ss are not only taking ownership of their learning process; they are authentically investing in the learning of their peers.

Conclusion: My students successfully built an innovative learning culture and are now equipped with a genuine understanding of WHY our curriculum is relevant to their life. Tomorrow, we begin the official process of second language acquisition.

I'm humbled to play a small role in the process, and I'm thankful to the people who have facilitated my learning.

Olentangy Local School District Closing the Achievement Gap:

The Pursuit of Perfection

Our current academic achievement levels are just the tip of the iceberg. Educators are in a constant chase of perfection, as we seek to maximize students' learning. The massive barrier to perfection is the evasive Achievement Gap, which continues to persist across generations. The most academically underperforming students are categorized as subgroups (African-American, Latino, Special Education and students in poverty).

There is not one clear solution to deep-dive the iceberg, the solution will require a clear focus on establishing learning conditions and robust practices. The Achievement Gap can only narrow once schools make an effort to address the culture and climate conditions for learning, coupled with consistent student engagement practices. A two-pronged approach, such as this, can yield higher than average results for ALL students. Changing the culture and human behavior, for both teachers and students, is the critical first step. Below are feasible actions schools can take to help change the learning culture and close the achievement gap.

LET'S GO BIG!

Closing the Achievement Gap comes down to three essential culture and climate conditions:

1. B- Belonging- It can't be stated enough; school and classroom learning conditions have to be caring and inviting. The learners have to feel connected to the school and their teachers. Most schools that excel at this have a "family type" of relationship with the students and parents. Some schools believe that personalized relationships with students and families are "the make or break" aspects of their school culture. Personalization does not mean that structure, organization, and toughness are out of the window. In schools that close the achievement gap, most students demand that their teachers are tough on them when they are not performing up to the expectations; this is when students know that the teachers care about them. This feeling of belonging is important because it leads students to personalize and engage with the academic content. When students feel like they belong in the organization (school), the levels of efficacy and learning expectations increase tremendously.

2. I-Intensity- Students believe that learning is more engaging when the learning ecosystem is focused and busy, in a meaningful way. In these focused classrooms, the teachers set the "minute-to-minute learning pace." Time on task becomes a respected asset by the students. In these highly intense learning ecosystems, there is zero downtime, and the learners often say "it's so fun" and "time flies in that class." Industriousness for learning becomes the norm, especially beyond the boundaries of the school walls. Intensity requires a level of organization and a keen hyper-focus on the instructional tasks. The number one predictor of expected outcomes is the task we assign to the students. "Task Predicts Performance"-Richard F. Elmore-Harvard University Instructional Core

3. G-Grit- failure at a task is part of the learning process. Teachers often provide various explanations of content when learners are confused or lack mastery of the content. Re-teaching, to clarify students' confusion, is an essential aspect of the terms resilience and industriousness. Not giving up on complicated tasks and finding different ways to solve problems are essential skills in fortifying personal Grit.

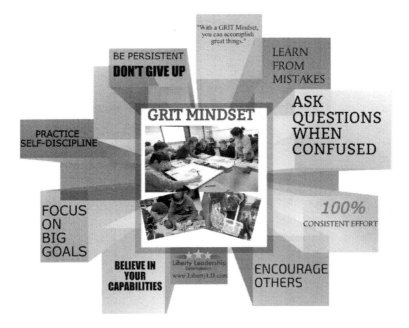

Once the culture and climate conditions are established, consistent student practices must occur.

The State Content Standards provide teachers with "what" specific sequence of content to teach. However, there is a lack of clarity on "how" to implement the content standards, for learners to demonstrate mastery orientation. The critical "how" becomes the learning tasks the teachers ask students to demonstrate in action. Students must create performance-based, real world, solutions for current or unknown problems.

THE 10,000-HOUR RULE

Grit and Perfection

Malcolm Gladwell's book, Outliers, prescribes to the notion that success is not just about intellectual capacity. Success requires the individual to practice specific tasks for 10,000 hours, to gain mastery orientation of the task. In education, we still have a vast majority of students and teachers attempting to prescribe the "10,000-hour practice rule" to an antiquated Education 1.0 model. Schools are spending more time on practicing and remembering skills, instead of applying and creating new skills. Not only does one need 10,000 hours on the task, the quality and rigor of the task matters. Quality learning outcomes are solely dependent upon the rigor of the instructional tasks teachers provide for the learners. Rigor is not a matter of learners doing more; rigor is clarity of focus on students owning and applying the learning to their real world problems.

The typical 180-day school year will provide students with 6 hours per day of formal instruction, accumulating 1080 hours at the end of each school year. So, the 10,000-hour rule is attainable in 9.3 years of formal academic learning (the start of high school). In those 9.3 years, students have to harvest the most rigorous learning possible.

Based on the current U.S. academic performance data, student learning is still stuck in Education 1.0 and demonstrate limited signs of moving forward. Enhancing the learning conditions and practices takes transformational leadership and a commitment to retraining educators and learners. Rebooting the education system requires a grit mindset, in the pursuit of perfection. 10,000 hours of perfect practice focuses on the individual's perspective, perseverance, and self-growth. Therefore, learners engaged in sustained, rigorous learning tasks will more than likely demonstrate higher levels of mastery orientation in their learning outcomes.

CHAPTER 5: DATA-DRIVEN

"You create your life, and you can recreate it, too. Look deep inside yourself to fathom the sort of life you really want to lead and the talents and passions that can make that possible."

-Ken Robinson

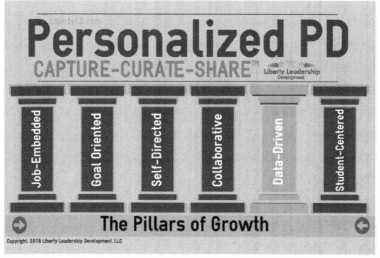

Contributing authors, Tyrone Olverson, MS
Carolyn B. H. Rogers, PhD

Data is a staple when you are actively engaged in the Grind! You have heard the saying *A picture may be worth a thousand words,* but for educators data-driven instruction provides the direction for what students know and should be able to do.

We choose to plant the seed!

Education is not the piling on of learning, information, data, facts, skills, or abilities - that's training or instruction - but is rather making visible what is hidden as a seed.

-by Thomas More

BOOST GRADUATION RATES

Using iGPS as your systemic tool

The charge has been very clear for decades. American high schools have to increase students' on-time graduation rates and decrease the dropout rate. For the U.S. to meet the requirements of a highly educated and skilled workforce of the future, career and college readiness matriculation are essential for economic security. Career and college-readiness sound like a very clear proposition that could be accomplished by every high school. The recent national high school graduation rate data demonstrates the largest gains in three decades. However, the high school dropout rate of over 514,000 students for the class of 2010 cohort is extremely high and comes at an economical cost to every community. The Alliance for Excellence (2011) estimates that each high school dropout student cost the nation $260,000 of lifetime social service for that student, which is a total of $133.64 billion for the class of 2010 dropouts. A decade of such trends will cost over $1.3 trillion, which is an unsustainable expenditure.

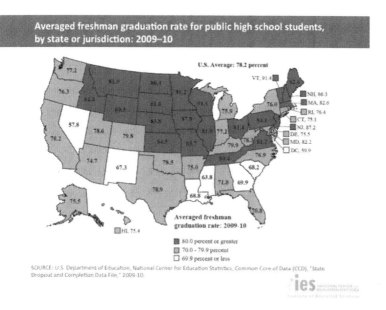

Averaged freshman graduation rate for public high school students, by state or jurisdiction: 2009–10

SOURCE: U.S. Department of Education, National Center for Education Statistics, Common Core of Data (CCD), "State Dropout and Completion Data File," 2009-10.

Solving the problem using the iGPS…

There is a sense of urgency with limited practical recommen-dations for success. Personalization seems to be a resonating theme and slogan; however, there is a lack of substance when seeking to translate personalization to results.

As a school administrator, a tool I've created and found to be very successful is the Intervention Graduation Positioning System (iGPS). The iGPS is a deinstitutionalized tool, and teachers provided valued input in the creation and application of the tool. With great success, I've used the iGPS tool in several types of school districts from urban to suburban. The iGPS tool provides a practical, quantitative system of metrics that teachers and schools can use to identify students' progress toward graduation or real-time interventions.

Personalization through the iGPS creates a disruptive innovation by quantifying students' cognitive assessments, motivation, and social fit data, to decrease the high school dropout rate. The iGPS categories are not part of the state or national graduation rate measurements, but practitioners have recognized that these categories have a direct effect on their school's graduation rate. The application of multiple data measures can create a hyper focus on the critical items responsible for an increase or decrease in both high school graduation and dropout rates.

How does the iGPS work?

The iGPS Matrix

1 point = +1.5 year over age for grade level

2 point = 2 or more days of out of school suspensions

3 point = more than ten absences in this school year

4 point = expulsion from school (14-180 days of missed instruction)

5 point = 1.0 or less GPA (4.0 scale) or 2 or more F's in a grading period

6 point = reading/math indicators (Standardized State Assessment)

There are 21 total points possible. Students with a total of 10+ total points need mandatory intervention.

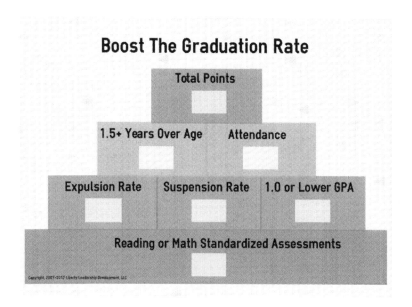

Schools do not have to wait to create interventions. Proactive data analysis can create a real-time assessment of progress toward graduation.

1. Cognitive Assessments

- If a student did not pass the Standardized State Assessment; continue to investigate the student profile.

Reading or Math Standardized Assessment Scale scores have the heaviest point total because the goal is to create a graduate who can demonstrate cognitive skills required for college and career-readiness. The first step of targeted intervention for all students must start with summative assessment data and performance indicators.

2. Motivation

- If a student missed 14-190 days of instruction due to suspension or expulsions and have a 1.0 or lower GPA; continue to investigate the student profile.

Student motivation plays a critical role in the education process. Teachers will have an opportunity to make a positive impact on the learning process if the students demonstrate a level of motivation. Students often suspended from school or demonstrating a lackluster grade point average require targeted intervention.

3. Social Fit

- If a student is 1.5 years over age for the grade level and does not attend school regularly; continue to investigate.

There is an issue of social fit when a student is 18+ months older than the cohort. Often the older students struggle with peer relations due to the age difference and interest levels. The older students can be provided with appropriate social outlets while maintaining enrollment status.

The graphic illustrates how the iGPS works. Data is input into appropriate categories, resulting in a final score. The points are viewed in a spreadsheet format for easier calculation.

Last Name	School	Gender	Eth	GPA	MATH INTV.	SP. ED code	LEP	% Math assess missed	Total Risk Pts
Smith	East	M	W	3.385		TBI	N	**60.0%**	11
Smith	West	F	W	3		SPH	N	42.9%	11
Smith	South	F	A	3.867		SLD	N	**50.0%**	14
Smith	North	F	B	2.769		SLD	N	57.1%	6
Smith	East	F	W	2.071		NON	N	28.6%	14
Smith	West	F	B	2.692		SLD	N	60.0%	16
Smith	South	M	B	0.643		NON	N	66.7%	19
Smith	North	M	W	2.214		NON	N	60.0%	15
Smith	East	M	W	2.133		NON	N	14.3%	11
Smith	West	M	B	2.077		NON	N	**60.0%**	5
Smith	South	M	B	1.385		NON	N	50.0%	14

Smith	North	F	H	1.643		NON	N	**50.0%**	1
Smith	East	M	B	0.444		NON	N	**66.7%**	19
Smith	West	M	W	2.556		SLD	N	50.0%	11
Smith	South	M	B	3		SLD	N	20.0%	11

THE PROOF IS IN THE PUDDING- THE REVIVAL

Increasing the high school graduation rate

The U.S. Department of Education (USDOE) released the 2009-10 school year's high school graduation rate. The data indicated a substantial rise (78.2%) in the graduation rate for all ethnic groups since the record high rate (73.4%) in 2005-06.

This increase in high school graduation rate helps to produce a generation of academically skilled workers to meet the demand of 21st Century jobs. Most importantly, the data demonstrates an increase in graduation rates as states attempt to close the achievement gap between minority students (African-American and Latino / Hispanic) and white students.

I had a great opportunity to work with Austin-East High School in Knoxville, Tennessee. The school is 90 percent African-American, 10 percent white and 83 percent socio-economically disadvantaged. The USDEO data documents a 2003-2010 State of Tennessee graduation rate trend, indicating that this particular high school's graduation rate was 10 percent below the state average of 63 percent in 2003. By 2010, Austin-East's graduation rate rose to a record number and finished 5 percent above the State of Tennessee's average graduation rate of 80 percent.

Austin-East High School was on the brink of falling under state control, but made tremendous gains in changing the school culture and practices. The work created a specific focus that all students must graduate with a college and career learning experience. The unintended consequence was that students graduated with a higher level of efficacy and resolve, as they entered college or a career.

The culture of Austin-East High School changed when teachers and students demanded more rigorous learning opportunities. Advanced Placement (AP) course enrollment soared from 3% to 36%. More students graduated with the skills required to attend college and be prepared for the workforce. *Personalization* was the focal point of the school's redesign initiative.

Personalized Teaching and Learning Focus Areas:

- Student advisory system focused on student academic behaviors.

- Personalized student growth plans.

- Cross-curricular and content specific time for teachers to collaboratively focus on student learning outcomes.

Academic Interventions

- Using academic data, identify students at risk of not graduating (i.e. standardized assessments, school attendance patterns, under credited, etc.)

- Alternative academic intervention programs (night school, credit recovery, interventions built into the school day, after school tutoring)

- Positive behavior supports

- Daily attendance incentive

Positive Behavior Recognition

- Parental/Community Engagement

- Academic growth recognition

- State of the school, led by students and teachers

College Access

- College tours
- College/university partnership
- College entrance preparatory course
- Increase in Advanced Placement course offerings
- Early college application process

ADVANCED PLACEMENT LEARNING CULTURE – FOCUS ON WHY, BEFORE WHAT

Create A Reader's Rap:

Start with the reader's rap as the foundation for your change initiative. The premise is to choose research literature that deals with the enduring topic your school would like to explore; the why. There are many books and research literature that resonate with the essential questions that many schools have; the problem is that schools do not explore the concepts of the literature with a complete sense of depth. The reader's rap provides the school with an opportunity to focus on the key concepts of the literature and focus on the actions associated with the desired change.

These levels of depth and breath should be part of the school culture. These attributes are school leadership issues that must be addressed in a collaborative manner. Schools are inundated with fad initiatives, in which teachers develop initiative fatigue. Many teachers join the "flavor of the month" initiatives presented by their school district. The reader's rap creates a focal point for schools as the leadership team, and teachers collectively seek to address issues of concern.

The clear communication of high expectations to students was the key item the leadership team discovered during the reader's rap investigation. The school decided to embark on creating student focus groups and focus on discovering students' levels of ambition, their personal goals, levels of efficacy and hope to discover insight to students' perceptions of their learning environment. The learning team asked random students, who were representative of the school, to anonymously answer the following questions (Adopted from the Tripod Project).

(Definition: When people feel "ambitious," it usually means that they intend to try hard to do really well. However, if they feel "ambivalent," it often means that they feel undecided about how hard to try.)

Sentences completed by students:

1. When I HAVE HIGH GOALS for achievement in a class, I think it is often because:

- At first, my parents just encouraged me and pushed me to do my best. Then I started to make and set goals for my life. Because of these goals, I have worked hard and I have done my best to achieve them. Also, teachers, friends, and my parents have encouraged me not to be a second rate citizen.

- I hate to fail, and there's some pressure from my parents to do well in school.

- I plan on taking classes in the future and feel that I need a strong foundation in that area.

- I like the teacher and/or the subject or I have friends in the class.

- My grades in that class aren't very good.

- I like the class and the people in it.

- I want to succeed.

- I want to get good grades so I can get a good job when I'm older.

- I enjoy the class. When I am in class, I understand and enjoy, and I want to do well. I also think that I have high goals for achievement in a class because I want to succeed in life. I believe that if I work hard now, it will help me get into a good school.

- When I make a goal, I stick with it, and sometimes I get little distractions, but I try not to, and if I get off track, I try to get back on.

- The class is something worthwhile. I'm not going to try my best in a class that isn't affecting my future or challenging me.

- I want to pass the class, so my parents don't get angry.

2. When I feel AMBIVALENT (wishy-washy or undecided) about my goals for achievement in a class, I think it's often because:

- My goals are typically higher than my peers'; so when I look at them and their goals I get discouraged, which opens the door to procrastination and undecided.

- I have obstacles in my way making getting to my goal a little bit harder.

- I don't care and I have to prioritize my life and classes.

- I don't like the teacher or subject, or I have no friends in the class.

- I don't think I could do much better in that class.

- I don't like the class and it's boring.

- I don't like this class or maybe it's so hard.

- The class is too hard or I'm just not interested in what we're learning about.

- I think it's because the class is too easy or I don't care about it. If I'm in a class that I think I'll do easily in, I don't set goals for myself.

- I don't understand how to go about doing something.

- I feel stagnated. The class is busy work; I'm not learning.

- I don't like the class or the way it's taught.

3. Some ways that my teachers ENCOURAGE me to have high goals for achievement are:

- They encourage me, even if I am not doing well. They are real about my strengths and weaknesses and always try to help me do my best, even in my weakest areas.

- They make me do things that are out of my comfort zone.

- They call on me in class, both when they think I know the answer or when I don't.

- They make the class fun and hands on.

- They tell me that I can do it and help me through the process.

- Giving extra credit or any other type of award.

- They help me, make things look easier than they are, give me tips and advice.

- They tell me things about how important good grades are and tell me to do better.

- Working hard will help you to get good grades. My English teacher rewarded me for working hard by nominating me for Breakfast Club and an English award. I was also nominated and became Science Student of the Month for my high achievement last year.

- They tell me I got talent, all I need is patience. Just basically telling me that I can do it, whatever it might be.

- Be serious with me. I'm not a little kid, so don't tell me this is important because you say so. My education is important to me, so show me how what you're teaching is good for my future.

- They know what I'm capable of and they know I can achieve things I set my mind to.

4. Some ways that my teachers help students to RECOVER their ambition after they've begun to feel ambivalent are:

- They offer advice and counsel. They will speak to me one-on-one, and then, if necessary, they will speak with my parents and me. They will help me set goals and help me to achieve them.

- They tell them to try a different way that will make it easier for them.

- They give the class time to work or read and go to the student and give them on-on-one time.

- They encourage them to come in for help at lunch, and they select them out for extra help during class.

- They try to give them self-confidence and help them recover.

- Make the class more fun.

- Encourage them, set some goals for them and try to help them and tell them what to do.

- Tell them it's not that hard and encourage them to try harder.

- They come over to ask them if they need help in the class. This often happens in math after I've done bad on a test. Teachers will also try to mix it up and throw in something fun to get students dedicated again.

- They show me how to get around my problem. They don't do it for me; they show me how to do it.

- Try to show why I should work hard. I'm old enough to know what I need to do to prepare for college, so give me something worthwhile to do.

- Take time to work with the student alone.

5. Some ways that a TEACHER might UNINTENTIONALLY DISCOURAGE a student from having high goals for achievement (in a particular class) are:

- Tell them that their question is stupid. They might allow other students to put down the discouraged student. They might not promote a positive classroom environment.

- They let them drop the class or let them stay in their comfort zone.

- The teacher laughs at a question or stops trying to answer a question because they can't think of a new way to explain the problem.

- They do not give a time for the student to come in for help or they disregard the students that are obviously falling behind.

- They joke around with them about it, but the student doesn't take it as a joke.

- Grading unfair. Not taking the time to explain things well.

- The teacher doesn't help that student and puts him/her down with his/her work.

- They tell them they're wrong or stupid. Or they tell them they aren't doing good in that particular class or just make fun of them.

- If a teacher makes a class sound too hard/easy, a student is less likely to apply himself because they figure their grade is set anyway.

- They ignore everything the student says and don't consider the class from a student's point of view.

- Busy work.

- The teacher spends time yelling at them all the time and talking down to them and not giving them a chance and not giving encouragement.

6. Finally, one more question: Do you feel ambivalent in some subjects but ambitious in others? Why or why not? What makes the difference?

- I have often felt that in math classes, in particular. I have never felt encouraged fully to do my best. I think this is because when I did study for a test, I would get it back and do bad. This would happen repeatedly, and I would get no encouragement, and so I would be continually discouraged. When I understood the material, doing well on tests, and was encouraged by the teacher and had a positive and fun learning environment.

- I feel ambitious in all of my subjects except math because that's the only class that I don't understand the most. Math has always been difficult for me.

- I think it depends on the class. If I'm in an honors class, I work hard because I want to appear smart to the other smart kids. On the other hand, in a "non-honors" class, it's bad to stand out and be ambitious because they look down on you.

- I love history because my teacher is fun and young and someone I can relate to, but I hate math because my teacher is distant and unable to control her class.

- No, because I'm doing almost the same in all my classes and all my teachers are good and help me a lot when I have problems which make it easier.

- Yes, it depends on the class and how it is run.

- Yes, because I like some classes and I hate others.

- I feel ambivalent in history because I usually don't do very well in it, but in all my other classes I'm ambitious. I usually do well in all my other classes.

- I'm very ambitious in History because I've always done well in that class. I'm also ambitious in Spanish because in that class I've always had high grades. I feel ambivalent in Math because it is one of my tougher classes. It seems like I always get the same grade every year – a B.

- Yes, because I might not understand a class or what the point of the class is. What makes the difference is what the student is interested in. Like me – some of the stuff in Math I don't understand why we need it, so I am ambivalent, but in Art, I'm not.

- Yes, the teacher can make a difference. If I respect my teacher, I'll work a lot harder than if I don't respect them.

- Yes, it all depends on the class and how the teacher teaches it.

The focus group sessions can force the learning community to be more innovative regarding teachers' approach to discovering students' class-to-class experiences. The goal of discovering students' class-to-class experiences is for teachers to communicate across subject areas. High school teachers are the content specialist; this process of discovering students' class-to-class experiences does lead to enhance collegial conversations.

These collegial conversations propel teachers' self-reflection of their instructional practices. Through self-reflection, teachers can become more innovative in their delivery of instruction and their ability to create interactive learning experiences for students.

The course reflection tool provides students with the opportunity to self-reflect on their role as the learner. It is seldom that schools formally ask students their opinions about their experience in the class. Schools might ask students about their thought of the teacher and the instruction provided, but it is seldom that schools would ask students about the role the learner played in the classroom. This is a bold approach because the school is asking the student to hold him/herself accountable for becoming an active participant in the learning process. With such a tool, students are expected to be active learners, instead of passive recipients of information. The reflection tool focus on students' levels of efficacy:

1. **Asking students to reflect on how they demonstrated learning**

2. **The relevance and application of the material**

3. **The students' perceptions of their learning**

Educators do a great job assessing students and work very hard to make sure their students are successful in life. It is fair to say that educators work very hard on isolated islands of greatness. The goal for teachers would be to create a systemic push where everyone is on the same page regarding students' expectations and providing academic rigor across all classrooms. Creating such a common purpose can be accomplished if the school leadership team provides the learning community with the essential tools required to maintain a cohesive, focused agenda. Schools need to include the students in the process of evaluating the learning experience.

Utilizing tools that provide information at a glance can be seen on two forms: Student Academic Course Evaluation Form (Appendix C) and Students' Evaluation of Their Learning Experience (Appendix D). Both forms provide teachers with a document for data driven instruction.

THE IDENTIFICATION OF THE RIGOROUS COURSES

As schools begin to create strategic plans for assessing their students' participation in rigorous courses, data is essential. This process of an equity audit can produce the stunning result of which student enroll in Honors/College Prep level courses and which students are marginalized in courses that do not challenge them academically.

The course request process will require schools to identify all of their current Honors/College prep and analyze current student enrollment trends. Schools having the ability to self-audit their courses is a significant step in the process because teachers, students, and the school leadership team will be held accountable to demonstrate the importance of certain courses. Most importantly, schools will have to articulate why certain students are enrolled in more rigorous courses, and others are not. This self-reflection aspect at the various levels of the learning environment can indeed change the functioning of the learning team.

What can be found:

The samples from one high school helped the learning team realize that their academically capable students were not enrolling in honors level courses. Students were taking the easy way out, not because teachers did not care, because there was no system in place to investigate students' course selections. The learning team from this high school was able to realize that fewer students were enrolling in Honors Math and Social Studies courses. The Science Department was able to realize that over half of the student body self-selected to enroll into the various Honors Science courses. This honors course matrix provided some clarity of course selection trends for all core academic departments.

The Social Studies Department was able to realize that they did not offer honors level courses to 10th-grade students, as the Science Department does. The Social Studies Department realized that they cater to the students in 11th and 12th-grade Advanced Placement (AP) courses, but do not provide the honors background for students in the lower grades. The Social Studies Department was also able to affirm that they will accept all students in AP courses as long as the students are willing to enroll and try. There is no mandatory prerequisite "right of passage" for students.

The English Department was the only academic department that required a summer project "right of passage," for students to be enrolled in Honors English courses. This process created a dilemma for many students who enrolled in summer school to free up their academic schedule during the school year. In this school, a majority of students took the required physical education classes during the summer, for them to have space in their schedule for their fine arts elective (band or orchestra).

The typical band students would:

1. Take a summer school physical education course

2. Attend mandatory marching band practice

3. Attend band camp

4. Family vacation

5. Maintain a summer job

6. Fulfill the National Honors Society recommendations for summer community service hours

The English Department had to deliberate on the purpose of the required summer project. Most of the summer project entailed reading a few books and providing a written report of the text. Upon asking some of the middle school English teachers, most of them said that they have students that could complete that project before leaving middle school. Students, particularly band students, hesitate to sign up for Honors English course because their summer schedule was so demanding.

The students were more than capable of completing the course work but simply did not have the time in the summer to fit that additional work into their hectic schedule.

This scenario and open dialogue encourage the educators to provide challenging learning opportunities for all students. See Appendix E for data-driven course information.

WHO ARE THEY AND HOW DO WE CHALLENGE THEM?

The task became very simple and focused; who are the students and how does the learning team build a system that demands high levels of excellence from every student? The Academic Matrix is built to identify every student and the current courses they are taking. The premises is to identify the students that are currently enrolled in Honors course and be sure that they continue to enroll in Honors, AP or Dual Enrollment Post-Secondary courses as the students matriculate through the academic curriculum.

Once students are identified in their current course, teachers will have the ability to have departmental conversations about the individual needs of students. Teachers will be able to identify students who excelled or struggled with certain course material and present this information to the following year's teachers. The learning team is building a bridge for teachers and students. This bridge allows teachers to focus on the presentation of content and the academic needs of the individual students.

All Honors level students are not on the same academic continuum.

Digging through the data can reveal the trends of various demographic student groups. Schools can assess if gender bias exists in certain courses or if there are disproportionate representations of students in different honors courses. This Academic Matrix provides the instructional leadership team and the entire building with more focus on the learning opportunities for students and the instructional practice that occur within those courses.

CHAPTER 6: STUDENT-CENTERED

"Your work is going to fill a large part of your life, and the only way to be truly satisfied is to do what you believe is great work. And the only way to do great work is to love what you do. If you haven't found it yet, keep looking. Don't settle. As with all matters of the heart, you'll know when you find it."

-Steve Jobs

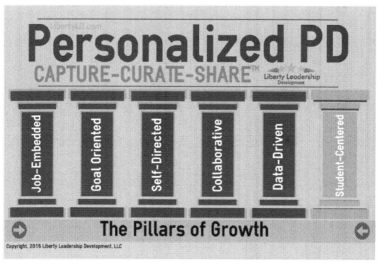

Contributing authors, Carolyn B. H. Rogers, PhD
Melissa Eddington
Vrondelia "Ronnie" Chandler

Student-centered is an active ingredient in the Grind! Yet, student-centered learning does not happen without strong relationships.

We choose to take the GRIND!

True teachers are those who use themselves as bridges over which they invite their students to cross; then, having facilitated their crossing, joyfully collapse, encouraging them to create their own.

– Nikos Kazantzakis

A CAREER BUILT ON STRONG RELATIONSHIPS

As I look back over my years in public education, many examples of Trust vs. Mistrust stage comes to mind. However, it was my kindergarten teachers in Columbus, Ohio that paints the clearer picture:

> Miss Dunlap has 29 eager and not so eager students in her class the first day of school. In fact, that number could be doubled with the apprehensive parents of the spirit filled 5-year-olds in her classroom. As I monitored the building, I stopped in her room just long enough to hear her tell the parents, "It is okay for you to remain with your child if you are feeling a bit unsure and uneasy. You see, I have been in your shoes with my daughter. You do not know me yet; therefore, you do not know if you can trust me. I promise to show you how much I love your child; and how smart I will help them to

become. You will see evidence of my love for your child when they learn colors, ABC, words, and poems.....As she continued to talk, you saw relief replace the fear that was in their face. In fact, more than half the parents started leaving the room.

Those parents had formed a level of trust for the teacher. However, that feeling of trust was not evident in all the classrooms:

> *I left Mrs. Dunlap's room feeling on top of the world. She was exhibiting the behavior I expected for all my teachers. Within steps of the next kindergarten classroom, I overheard several parents grumbling as they passed me in the hall. I immediately stopped them to find out what The first mother spoke of how the teacher would not let them stay with their child. The other mother was in tears as she spoke of the first time she has been away from her daughter.*

In this case, they immediately had a level of mistrust for the second kindergarten teacher. I will use Erik Erikson's Stages of Psychological Development (Erikson, 1950) to articulate my growth as an educational professional. These stages helped guide my leadership and development.

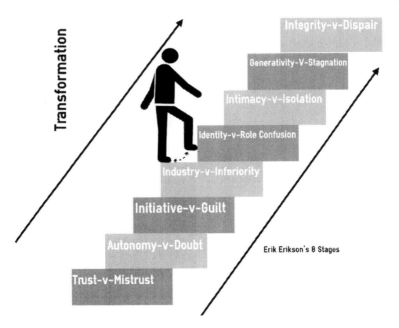

(Graphic by Saul McLeod)

Stages	Attributes of the Stages	Classroom Attributes
Autonomy vs. Shame	Autonomy and will power can be developed; the student's self-explore his or her world (building toward relevance in learning).	Autonomy and will power can be developed; the student's self-explore his or her world (building toward relevance in learning).

As a student I can clearly remember being in Mrs. Goodson's classroom when the clarity was so real, she was teaching us to write short stories. She wanted us to visualize the character.

She made each of us close our eyes, and she asked questions, read passages, and even sung a song to bring the character to life in our mind. When she told us to open our eyes, she asked us to begin writing what we saw without discussing it with the other students. The next day, she had us to read our stories aloud to the class. It was the reading aloud that I remembered understanding how we all see things from our vantage point, yet we all saw this activity as relevant to current and future learning.

Stages	Attributes of the Stages	Classroom Attributes
Initiative vs. Guilt	Child is striving to find purpose and positive self-worth.	Students take the initiative self-select how they learn.
The Industry vs. Inferiority Stage	The need to demonstrate competence in regards to the basic skills of school; developing a sense of self	Students have multiple opportunities to develop their skills and demonstrate their skills to peers.

During the early stages of being a school principal, I was always in and out of the classrooms. This practice was before learning about the formalized Walk-through protocol; I was simply in the room to understand what the children were learning and how the teachers were teaching.

I was in the classrooms so often that the students soon learned to keep working when I came into the classroom. Well, on this particular day, you could tell this little boy was waiting for me to show up. As soon as I walked into the room, his little hand shot up in the air. The teacher rushed over to him and whispered into his ear. He yelled, "Not you…HER!"

Before I could make it over to him, the teacher stepped in my path and said, "He doesn't want anything. He is always questioning me, and now he wants to bother you." I thanked her but immediately moved over to the boy to find out what he had to say. When I reached him, he said, "Maybe you can tell me why we have to read these baby books when we already know how to read chapter books. I asked my teacher, and she keeps saying I do not know everything in the story. Well, she is wrong, because I do. I have read three different versions of The Three Bears and every time that little girl gets in the baby's bed…."

Well by now, I cannot keep a straight face, but I immediately knew that this child was trying to find purpose in the assignment, and he was trying to take the initiative to increase his level of learning.

After that visit, I worked with the teacher to develop learning centers for all children to have multiple opportunities to develop their skills. This story provides an opportunity for the teacher to assess this student's competency level since the student had obviously demonstrated his skills to the teacher and peers in the class.

A week later in the cafeteria, the same student ran up to me and showed me a list of reading books he is going to check out at the library. He said, "My teacher gave me some kind of reading test and then she gave me a list of books that I might be interested in reading."

Stages	Attributes of the Stages	Classroom Attributes
Identity vs. Role Confusion	Testing boundaries. Develop a new sense of identity and self in regards to one's purpose, future, and meaning in life.	Students have the opportunity to grow as they learn new and relevant content.

I was a fifth-grade teacher in a rural area of a South Carolina school district. I worked hard to make sure my students were self-sufficient and did not let the area define who they were and what they could do. I came to school every day and took pride in myself for having high achieving students. However, tragedy struck my best friends younger sister requiring me to go to Connecticut for a funeral. As soon as I found out, I went to the principal to request a substitute.

He granted me permission, and I proceeded to get things ready for the substitute. In doing so, I summoned all of my students to let them know where I was going and why and to remind them of their roles, responsibilities, and behaviors in my absence.

Fifth graders in this self-contained class were the best helpers in the world. I had classroom librarians, line leaders, playground assistants, bulletin board designers, reading and math tutors, and the like. All of my students were responsible for something, and each of them took their jobs seriously. As I left that evening, I was sure they would live up to my high expectation of being exceptional students.

Well five days later, I returned to find a note in my box to see the principal before going to my room. I entered the office thinking something had happened to one of my children. I was very anxious. To my surprise, it was not my children, but me who was the problem. My principal was upset with me because I failed to call a substitute.

Confused, I reminded him that he gave me permission to leave. It was then that he realized that I had never been absent from school in the two years he had worked with me, so I was not familiar with the process of calling a substitute. We both laugh as he showed me the information in the handbook. However, the story does not end there.

My principal proceeds to tell me that he did not know that I did not have a substitute until the last day of my absence. My students held class, went out for recess, turned in the roll to the office, etc. It was only when they went to the cafeteria on day five of my absence that a substitute worker was in charge of the line and she would not let my cafeteria leader turn in the tickets. When the lady asked for her teacher, she informed her that I was in Connecticut. The worker sent for the principal.

This story is a prime example of how children can be successful at leading as they push boundaries. Each one of my students was able to develop a new sense of identity and self in regards to one's purpose for leadership that will aid them in the future.

Stages	Attributes of the Stages	Classroom Attributes
Intimacy vs. Isolation	The focus becomes the virtue of love.	Students develop a love for learning based previous experience.
Generativity vs. Stagnation	Builds upon the love and empathy.	Students establish a sense of reflective learning during their learning process.

When you get that "aha!" moment, it stays with you forever. I am sure you can remember the first time you rode a bicycle or heard a baby say his first word. As a classroom teacher, fortunately, I can remember many moments of success and student learning. On this particular day, I passed out the results of the spelling test. Henry, a nine-year-old second grader, was extremely cognitively low but so very happy to at school. He simply enjoyed life and the interactions with his peers.

My goal was not to have him repeat the second grade for the third year in a row. Henry had worked very hard learning his spelling and sight words. He would come early in the morning and beg to stay late in the afternoon. He refused to have a list of five words that I suggested. He wanted ten spelling words just like his classmates. What I decided was to teach Henry the values associated with each grade. He learned that an A was great, B was good, C was okay, D was not so good, and an F was bad. What he did not understand was the numerical value associated with the grade. I also decided that he did not need to know that information. Every Monday all of my students took a pre-test, and most of them had at least 50% of the words correct. Henry always made an F on Monday. However, with much teaching, tutoring, and practice, he would learn at least half of the words, which still equated to 50; which was an F.

Henry always cried when he got that F because he knew he had worked so very hard. With my new system, one words wrong was an A, 2 - 3 was a B, 4-5 words was a C, 6 was a D and 7 – 10 was an F. On the first Friday of our new grading system, when Henry got his spelling test it had a big blue C. He smiled the biggest brightest smile, then said "I passed. I am smart just like Callie."

Understand that Callie was the little girl who had tutored him faithfully for the past three months. I do not know who was happiest at that moment.

That day was the first of many successes for Henry. He had to learn how to experience success. He had many years of working hard but failed due to a system that did not reward efforts. Based on that one day of success, Henry developed a love for learning based on his success experience.

Stages	Attributes of the Stages	Classroom Attributes
Integrity vs. Despair	A time of reflection during which the virtue of wisdom can be obtained.	A feeling of satisfaction and attainment is prevalent.

As I was leaving home to attend college, I can remember clearly my granny's conversation about integrity. She looked me in the eyes and said, "Whatever you do in life, do not compromise your integrity. You need to love yourself so much that the only thing that can enter your life would be someone who loves you as much." She went on to say, "Trust will go along way. If you cannot trust the person you are with, then walk away. It will not cost you a thing."

In my role as a principal, those words became very meaningful. It was the graduation of one of my former fifth-grade students. He held a party at his home and invited me to attend. I had several other parties to attend, so I arrived at his house a bit late. When I walked around the side of the house to the backyard where about 100 guests were still mingling, I instantly spotted Quinton.

Our eyes met about the same time, and I heard his mother yell, "She's here! Everybody…She is here!" I had not a clue what was happening. After hugs from Quinton and his family, he asked everyone to quiet down because he had something to say. He held my hand and began to speak to my heart.

Quinton's Speech:

Today I am here with my family and friend because of my principal, Mrs. Rogers refused to let the system guide her heart. About seven years ago, my family was struggling with drugs and alcohol. There were days my sister, and I was not picked up from school. We would wait patiently by a bush knowing that my mom or pop may not be there to get us. Mrs. Rogers would come out to check on us. After what seemed like hours, I am sure it was less, she brought us in, gave us a snack and told us she would take us home. On most of those trips home, we would get there, and no one would be home. I later realized that she was supposed to call Children Services, but instead, she took us home with her son. We had a nice warm place to stay and warm a sit-down dinner with her family. I remember the warm family conversations at the dinner table and the caring family time shared. It happened so often that we stopped going out to the curve to wait on my parents. As I look back on those acts of kindness, I realize today may not have been possible without you, Mrs. Rogers. Today, my mother and father are clean. Those days of despair are no more. We love you.

At that moment there was not a dry eye in the place, including me. I do not advocate breaking the law. I simply say sometimes we have to know what hope looks like. In this situation, a feeling of satisfaction and attainment was prevalent.

COMMUNICATION & ENGLISH LANGUAGE LEARNER

Simple definition of COMMUNICATION according to Merriam-Webster's Dictionary:

- The act or process of using words, sounds, signs, or behaviors to express or exchange information or to express your ideas, thoughts, feelings, etc., to someone else

- A message that is given to someone: a letter, telephone call, etc.

Communication in any profession is important and necessary but even more so in education. We as educators are given someone's precious cargo every day to educate, so it is our responsibility to communicate with our families. The added challenge is when you work with families who speak other languages at home. Is it impossible to communicate with them? Absolutely Not! We may have to be more creative and look into different tools, but as professionals, it is our responsibility to make it happen.

Through communication with our families, we are building relationships; Relationships are key. The parent-teacher relationship is vital in any educational setting but more so when you are working with families from other countries. They could be new to the country and unsure how to navigate American schools. This is where the relationship with the classroom teacher and the ELL teacher comes into play. We need to create an environment that is comfortable to our families, so the transition is smooth.

I have been in education for almost 16 years, and the tools for communication have changed immensely over time. When I first began teaching, I sent a monthly newsletter home to my families to keep them informed. I can't tell you the last time I wrote a newsletter as I have changed my practice to change with the times and include different tools. We need to adjust our communication techniques based on our families and technologies.

Another thing to factor is the make-up of our families. Sometimes our ELL families are separated due to financial reasons or immigration challenges, so using the blanket term of "parents" may not be correct or could be offensive. Consider changing your verbiage to the family of (insert the last name) to prevent being incorrect or offensive.

There are many different tools educators can use to communicate with ELL families. Some tools are electronic while others are more traditional. Let's look at the some of the different communication tools used by ELL and classroom teachers alike.

When using electronic communication, it can be updated much more quickly and more often. Many of our ELL families have relatives in their native countries so the use of electronic communication can be shared with everyone all across the world. It does require the teacher and families to have some basic knowledge of technology tools, but many of these tools are very easy to use.

For example, Remind is a free communication tool that allows teachers to connect instantly with families and students through email, SMS or their free mobile app (available for iOS and Android). One of the great benefits of Remind is that you can now translate your messages into 90+ different languages. English and Japanese.

Twitter, Facebook, Instagram and other social media platforms are also electronic ways to communicate with families. Information can be pushed out quickly, and all members or subscribers can view it immediately. Social media can allow teachers to share their stories of their classrooms in a quick and efficient manner and our families have access as well.

Many teachers create weekly or monthly newsletters for families. They can highlight major topics being taught in each subject area, upcoming events and any other school-wide information. Some newsletters are sent home electronically while others send home hard copies. Newsletters are a great way to communicate with families, but the information is already old by the time it reaches home. Another downfall of newsletters is that some cannot be translated into other languages. If you are using newsletters to provide information, I encourage you to use a site that has translation capabilities.

Hosting a blog or creating a website is a great way to provide information for families. You have the ability to add pictures, videos, and other documents to share with families here and across borders. Students can go home and share more about the happenings of the day as well to further share the story.

My goal is to have my students be the writers for the classroom blog so that they can be the storytellers. They will also be able to write in their L1 (first language), so family members are guaranteed to understand.

If your families are unsure or apprehensive to use technology tools, hold a parent meeting either at your school or in their community to guide them through the sign-up process. Technology can be scary for some, so modeling for them can create a smooth introduction and in turn can help build relationships.

We have a beginning of the year meeting with all ELL parents and bilingual aides from the respective language groups. We cover US schools basics, district information but we also allow time for technology time. It's amazing what a little time, a few laptops and a few bilingual aides can do in the way of building relationships. We can update information for their children and show them how our communication methods work and how to use them.

Another obstacle with technology usage with families is the lack of smart phones or computers in the house. Not all of our families, especially our ELL families, may not have these devices in their home; therefore, they'd be unable to retrieve the information.

When we ONLY use electronic means to communicate, we can alienate our families. Written and oral communication can reach most, but can it be read and heard by all? The answer is sadly no...not all of our parents can read and write their L1 (first language), so we need to provide other means of communication.

We cannot communicate by electronic or written communication alone. We must also utilize oral communication with families. Oral communication can be heard by all; therefore no one is excluded.

ORAL COMMUNICATION

Oral Communication

Phone calls home are great ways to communicate with families especially those families that speak languages other than English. It is very simple to pick up the phone and share some information. What makes is more difficult is when the person on the other end of the phone does not speak the same language. Use bilingual aides or other staff members fluent in the other language to call home with you the teacher.

When calling home with the use of an interpreter, please have the interpreter state at the beginning of the phone call that they are on speakerphone and have them introduce you, the originator of the needed phone call communication. This allows the family member to feel safe with the people on the other end of the phone. I recommend using both languages to communicate with the family member to make sure there is no confusion.

An example phone call may go like this…

- Interpreter: Hello, Mrs. (insert name)…I am (insert name), the bilingual aide here at (insert name of school), and I have (insert teacher's name) with me. She wanted to talk to you about (insert child's name), and I am here to help with the translation of the conversation.

- Teacher: Hello, Mrs. (insert name). I wanted to talk to you about (state reason for the call).

The teacher will state the reason for the phone call then the interpreter will translate. The translator will listen to the answer, then translate it into English for you. Go back and forth like this until the conversation is finished. It may take a bit longer, but I feel it is worth the time it takes because each side feels that they are being heard. After the phone call is ended, write down a few notes along with the date and name of the interpreter and keep with your notes.

Documentation is needed for any and all communication with families. If a simple phone call is not enough to get the information presented, take the time to hold a family meeting. Invite the family in or if needed, go the family to continue the conversation. Sometimes families do not have transportation, so a simple ride to their house (home visits) to wrap up the conversation is necessary.

The wonderful aspect of meetings is that any number of people can attend. Sometimes we need a team approach to continue the conversation; therefore, a meeting would be necessary. During a meeting like this, I suggest delegating someone to be the note taker. After the meeting is over, share the notes with each participant so they can add any information. For this, I suggest using Google Docs to collaborate due to the ease of use.

Parent meetings are wonderful and helpful but can be overwhelming for some families. Anytime you are scheduling a meeting with parents; it's helpful to include in your conversation the number of people attending the meeting. It allows the families to prepare mentally for the upcoming meeting and allows them time to reconsider or ask for fewer people. Also, parent meetings with interpreters take much longer than meetings without interpreters. Please keep the families and staff members in mind when you are scheduling.

It doesn't matter whether or not you use electronic or written communication and/or oral communication, and it is vital for any educational relationship. Parents and teachers must work as a team to provide the best education for their children.

CONTRIBUTING MY VOICE

"The Turbulent Choice"

Authentic voices are sometimes hard to hear. Not because they are not speaking loudly enough but rather because they are raw and real. Kudos to Randall for keeping it real in "Welcome to the Grind." During the years 2008-2010 Dr. Randall Sampson provided transformative coaching for the administration and faculty of one of our Project GRAD high schools, Austin-East Magnet High School. His academic support was impactful, and our collaboration provided important connections.

Our work at Project GRAD Knoxville is a continuum of persistent connections with students and families that start at Kindergarten and continues into young adulthood as students complete high school and higher education. Our structure is depicted in the diagram.

Project GRAD Knoxville

Student and Family Support	College and Career Access	College and Career Success
• Parental involvement activities and workshops • Enrichment and group activities • Before and after-school programs • Access to community agencies • Tutoring and mentoring	• Academic review and tutoring • College visits and career exploration opportunities • College application assistance • Scholarship research and assistance • ACT preparation workshops for students and parents • Attendance and grade monitoring • Early awareness beginning in elementary school	• Financial literacy • Yearly FAFSA renewals • Access to college experiences through summer institutes and college panels • Job and internship opportunities • Scholarship claim assistance • Workshops and seminars

Full-time School-Based GRAD staff provides a variety of support that includes addressing barriers to success (including meeting basic needs), providing exposure and experiences that widen future options, and serving as a compass as students navigate the pathways to their dreams. This support lightens a load of classroom teachers and administrators as they focus on instructional time and of guidance staff who have multiple responsibilities.

Our higher education partners provide college institute experiences that provide a real life taste of college. Full-time College/Career Success Coaches then walk with our students (many of whom are first-generation college) as they pursue and persist through higher education. The scholars themselves give back as Pre-College Mentors for the University summer institute, serving as members of the GRAD College Board, and visiting GRAD K-12 schools as GRAD Alumni speakers.

159

Fourteen urban schools are served by Project GRAD Knoxville—two high schools, two middle schools, and ten elementary schools.

In Knoxville, we have seen the great impact because of a community-wide commitment to youth.

- The combined graduation rate for the two Project GRAD Knoxville high schools increased from 50% when we started our work in 2001 to 81% in 2015.

- The percentage of students enrolling in higher education has now increased from 30% to 57%. The number of students from Austin-East and Fulton enrolling at the flagship University of Tennessee-Knoxville has increased 400% since the Knox County Schools/GRAD partnership was established. Since start up, 4,098 Summer Institute on-campus experiences have been provided for Project GRAD scholars. The partnership by Pellissippi State Community College and the University of Tennessee-Knoxville proved to be a valuable gateway to college and career-readiness. As an additional partner, The Tennessee College of Applied Technology at Knoxville began offering a Summer Institute for GRAD Knoxville in June 2016.

- The average national postsecondary completion rate for students from low-income circumstances is 10%. Comparatively, the percentage of GRAD Knoxville completers is 47%. Four program alumni are now full-time staff members with Project GRAD Knoxville, providing the very support they once received.

If we want to engage students at the heart level--essential for a real relationship--, we have to care about them and listen to them. Our words can be life-giving or can crush their spirit. I had the honor of being the 2015 Commencement speaker for my community college alma mater. Following is that speech in its entirety. I hope you take from it a reminder that after you have listened to youth, the words you then speak in response deeply matter. Choose them carefully.

The Vrondelia Chandler 2015 Pellissippi State Community College Commencement Remarks May 13, 2015 is a must see. Additionally, the transcript is provided below.

https://www.youtube.com/watch?v=GJXaj2NhX1g

"The Turbulent Choice"

Thank you so much for this opportunity. I'm so proud to be an alum of this college! In fact, there are many of us in this arena today. If you are a graduate of Pellissippi State under any of our names -- State Technical Institute at Knoxville, Pellissippi State Technical Community College, Pellissippi State Community College--I want to ask you to stand and remain standing for just a moment. Wow – there are a bunch of us here. We need some kind of secret handshake or something!

Graduates, look around you. In just a short while you will join this number. All of us who are Pellissippi alum have an opportunity to help spread the message to other youth and adults that GREAT BEGINNINGS HAPPEN HERE! Our personal example of success shows that Pellissippi State is a first class, first choice, institution and NOT a last resort. Let us continue to be ambassadors for the Community College.

Thank you, Dr. Wise for this invitation. Dr. Wise is on my Board at Project GRAD (Graduation Really Achieves Dreams), and I was meeting with him a couple of months ago about creating a couple of college student opportunities with GRAD when he said, "there is a second thing I want to talk with you about today. I want you to be our Commencement speaker."

Have you ever had that moment when there is this delay in what your ears just heard and what your brain processes? That happened to me when Dr. Wise extended that invitation. I was listening and nodding. Then I thought, 'whoa, wait, what did he just say? He just asked me to speak at Pellissippi's Commencement! At Thompson-Boling Arena!' And it took me a moment to regain my composure.

Because this is an incredibly humbling blessing; I am honored to stand before all of you, in all of this. Because at the beginning of the path that led to this day, I never would have imagined this moment. A chain of choices led to this moment. And "choice" is what I want to talk about briefly today. I've titled my remarks "The Turbulent Choice."

And here is the point of everything I'm about to say summed up in one sentence. If you only write one note, if you only tweet one thing, if you only put one thing in your phone's note pad, write this: "Be at peace with your choice or make a new choice." I want the graduates to repeat that after me: Be at peace with your choice------or make a new choice-----.

I was in Philadelphia last week for a national Cities United meeting during the day of the Philadelphia protest rally and march. A lot was publicized in the national news about the march being on the brink of turning violent. Not so. It was an incredible and peaceful demonstration. The protesters were of all ages, genders, and ethnicities. The Mayor and police chief protected the marchers as citizens who have the First Amendment right to peaceful protest, but they also made it clear they were ready for anything else that popped off. An important fact Philadelphia local news reported that the mainstream did not report, was that the officers were required to read for themselves the First Amendment in advance of the protest so they would be mindful that the people had the right to assemble and to speak. Peaceful protest is a choice.

On my flight to Philadelphia, I was dozing and awakened to turbulence. I wasn't alarmed by that, I have flown several times. I took a minute to get my wits about me and figured out the direction we were going. You see, when you fly, turbulence occurs when you change altitude. Turbulence occurs when you are both ascending/going up, or descending/moving down. Remember that as the representation of a real life lesson. When you experience turbulence in your life, check your direction.

Are you going up or down? And if a regrettable choice is causing the turbulence and you have no peace, make a new choice.

I shared with Dr. Wise that I can still, in my mind, see the face of the high school teacher who looked at me with disgust when she found out I was going to be a teen mom. My teacher said to me "you were a smart girl, but now you'll never be anything." Those words hurt, but I chose NOT to believe her. And as an adult, I made the choice to FORGIVE her. And I've been married to that high school daughter's Daddy for 37 years and counting! We even have a precious, wonderful 11-year-old granddaughter. And I admit I intentionally chose to think about that high school moment last November when I officially moved into the role of Chief Executive Officer and Executive Director of Project GRAD!

Listen, don't waste your time with unforgiveness. It just makes you bitter and eats you up. You know the process of unforgiveness? Unforgiveness is like YOU drinking rat poison, and then waiting for the rat to die! It might be time to consider making a different choice.

Be at peace with your choice, or make a new choice.

Life is going to present to you a series of choices to be made as life moves on. Many of you have had to overcome some things to get to this point of graduation. I know what that is like. I have an amazing life, but I have not always been who I am.

I worked on my degrees as a working, non-traditional adult student with a husband, two kids, and a full-time job. And my personal life story includes dealing with family alcoholism, the early deaths of my parents, my husband's work-ending spinal injury when he was only 29, five years into our marriage. We dealt with several surgeries, having to fight for workers comp and social security and the pressures nearly ended our marriage. But we survived all that and life moved on. And then in 1991 the lowest moment of my life happened when we tragically lost our second daughter Sparkle just a few months before her 13th birthday to adolescent suicide. I was working at Pellissippi during the time of Sparkle's death, and I will be forever grateful for the way my coworkers loved and supported me through that time. Even surviving breast cancer 20 years later, didn't compare to the pain of losing my child.

What do you do when your life falls apart?

In all of those moments I just described, I had to make some tough new choices.

- I chose to continue to trust that God is sovereign and has a purpose for everything *He* allows into my life.
- I chose to continue to hope and to love.
- I chose to continue, to live, and not just survive. And there IS a difference!

I have lived long enough to know that time and energy are precious and limited. So pay attention to how you spend both time and energy. Every day is a gift. Don't use all of your time and energy fighting---reserve some to CREATE.

Now I know some people in here are squirming by now, and wondering "why is this CEO standing up there telling all her business?" There is a reason for my transparency.

There is a reason I chose to share with you what I call "My OTHER Resume"---and we all have one. I want you to remember that no matter what happens TO you, you always have the power to choose.

Be at peace with your choice or make a new choice.

What do you choose to reach for in your lowest moment?

Some reach for alcohol. Some reach for drugs. I reach for my faith. Someone once asked me 'what is your greatest business asset?' and I told them my greatest asset period, is my faith in the Lord Jesus Christ.

Don't get nervous I didn't come to preach to you. You have to make your choice with regards to spiritual peace. But just be sure that what you put your trust in can sustain you and give you peace in your lowest moments.

I also share my story because I want to encourage you to own ALL of who you are, and choose to be a principled leader. Leading from core values will serve you well as you make hard choices.

This is important because you must know that no matter what you do, somebody is not going to like it. And no matter what you do, somebody will tell you 'that's the wrong thing to do.' So, YOU must own your choices and lead according to your principles.

Be at peace with your choice or make a new choice.

Choice demands action. What will you do differently to BE different?

Finally, you must know that you are more than what you have been through--- or what you may be going through this very moment. You must know that low moments WILL pass and life will move on. This is not the end of your story. There is so much more for you. There is greatness in you, and I expect greatness from you!

Remember, you always have the ability to choose.

Be at peace with your choice, or make a new choice.

Thank you and congratulations.

REFERENCES

Alliance For Excellent Education: Issue Brief (2011, November). Retrieved from http://all4ed.org/wp-content/uploads/2013/06/HighCost.pdf

Brain Quote Nelson Mandela Quotes (2017). Retrieved from https://www.brainyquote.com/quotes/authors/n/nelson_mandela.html

Collins, J. C. (2001). *Good to great: Why some companies make the leap and others don't.* New York, NY: HarperBusiness.

Erikson, E.H. (1950). *Childhood and Society.* New York: Norton.

Ferguson, R.F. (2007). *Toward Excellence with Equity.* Harvard Education Press, Cambridge, MA

Fry, R. (2015) *Millennials Surpass Gen Xers as the largest generation in U.S. labor force.* Pew Research Center. Retrieved from http://www.pewresearch.org/fact-tank/2015/05/11/millennials-surpass-gen-xers-as-the-largest-generation-in-u-s-labor-force/

Gladwell, Malcolm, 1963-. (2008). *Outliers : the story of success.* New York: Little, Brown and Co.,

Gordon, Jon (2010). *Soup: A recipe to create a culture of greatness.* John Wiley & Sons: Hoboken, New Jersey

Inspiring Quotes by Lou Holtz (2017). Retrieved from http://quoteideas.com/lou-holtz-quotes/

Rise and Shine-Welcome To The Grind (2014, September 29). Retrieved from https://motivationmentalist.com/2014/09/29/rise-and-shine-welcome-to-the-grind/

U.S. Department of Education (2009-10), National Center for Education Statistics, Common Core and Data (CCD). "State Dropout and Completion Data File."

APPENDICES

APPENDIX A

ACT PREDICTOR

Student Name	Honors Course	Teacher	Ethnicity	Grade	GPA	ACT PLAN
Tammy	Env. Bio	Smith	Af-Amer.	10	2.6	16-20
Tammy	Env. Bio	Smith	Af-Amer.	10	2.74	16-20
Tammy	Env Bio	Smith	AA	10	2.74	16-20
Tammy	Cell Bio	Smith	AA	10	2.74	16-20
Tammy	Env. Bio	Smith	Af-Amer.	10	2.93	17-21
Tammy	Cell Bio	Smith	Af.-Amer.	10	2.93	17-21
Todd		Smith	Af-Amer.	10	3.122	22-26
Todd	Env. Bio	Smith	Af-Amer.	10	3.15	NA
Todd		Smith	Af-Amer.	10	3.162	NA
Todd	Chem.	Smith	AA	10	3.176	19-23
Todd		Smith	AA	10	3.19	17-21
Todd	Env. Bio	Smith	AA	10	3.2	15-19

Todd	Cell Bio.	Smith	AA	10	3.204	15-19
Todd	Chem.	Smith	AA	10	3.3	17-21
Todd		Smith	AA	10	3.3	18-22
Todd	AmLit/Com	Smith	AA	10	3.49	19-23
Todd		Smith	AA	10	3.5	13-17
Todd	AmLit/Com	Smith	AA	10	3.531	17-21
Shelly	**AmLit/Com**	**Smith**	**AA**	**10**	**3.531**	**17-21**
Shelly	**Env. Bio**	**Smith**	**AA**	**10**	**3.55**	**18-22**
Shelly	**Chem.**	**Smith**	**AA**	**10**	**3.61**	**26-30**
Shelly	**Chem.**	**Smith**	**Multi.**	**10**	**3.769**	**22-26**
Shelly	**ALG 2**	**Smith**	**Multi.**	**10**	**3.769**	**22-26**
Shelly	**Env. Bio**	**Smith**	**AA**	**10**	**3.96**	**19-23**
Shelly	**Cell Bio.**	**Smith**	**AA**	**10**	**3.96**	**19-23**
Shelly	**ALG 2**	**Smith**	**Multi.**	**10**	**3.962**	**23-27**
Shelly	**Env. Bio**	**Smith**	**Multi.**	**10**	**4.06**	**18-22**
Shelly	**AmLit/Com**	**Smith**	**Hispanic**	**10**	**4.39**	**29-33**

APPENDIX B

HONORS/COLLEGE PREP
COURSE ENROLLMENT

Student Name	HNR Sci.	HNR Math	HNR Eng.	HNR History	Teacher	Ethnicity	GPA	GRADE
John			X		Smith	AF-Amer.		9
John			X		Smith	AF-Amer.		9
John		X			Smith	AF-Amer.		9
John		X			Smith	MULTI		9
John			X		Smith	AF-Amer.		9
John		X			Smith	AF-Amer.		9
John			X		Smith	AF-Amer.		9

HONORS/COLLEGE PREP COURSE ENROLLMENT

Student Name	HNR Sci.	HNR Math	HNR Eng.	HNR History	Teacher	Ethnicity	GPA	GRADE
Kim	X				Smith	AF-Amer.		10
Kim	X				Smith	AF-Amer.		10
Kim	X				Smith	AF-Amer.		10
Kim			X		Smith	AF-Amer.		10
Kim	X				Smith	AF-Amer.		10
Student Name	HNR Sci.	HNR Math	HNR Eng.	HNR History	Teacher	Ethnicity	GPA	GRADE
Tom			X		Smith	AF-Amer.		11
Tom		X			Smith	AF-Amer.		11
Tom	X				Smith	AF-Amer.		11

Tom	X				Smith	AF-Amer.		11
Tom	X				Smith	AF-Amer.		11
Tom	X				Smith	AF-Amer.		11

APPENDIX C

STUDENT ACADEMIC COURSE
EVALUATION FORM

Course Title: _____

Date of Course: _____

Student Name : _____

How would you rate your participation in this course?	Excellent	Good	Fair	Poor
My participation in the discussions				
My participation in the group activities				
My contribution to the class objectives				

How would you rate presentation of the material?	Excellent	Good	Fair	Poor
Overall				
Lecture/Discussions				
Exercises/Activities				

How would you rate your demonstration of learning?	Excellent	Good	Fair	Poor
Overall				
Oral Presentation				
Written Reports				
Portfolio				

The learning in this class met my personal goals?	Agree	Neutral	Disagree

The information presented in this class was relevant to me	Agree	Neutral	Disagree
My real life			
Future job			

I will apply the information learned in this class to other classes?	Agree	Neutral	Disagree

Which types of learning exercises were most/least effective for you?	
Most effective	
Least effective	

APPENDIX D

STUDENTS' EVALUATION
OF THEIR LEARNING EXPERIENCE

1. Educational expectations were clearly explained?

   Strongly disagree ○○○○ Strongly Agree

2. Information provided about the relevance of this course was clear

   Strongly disagree ○○○○ Strongly Agree

3. Response to my questions in this class were handled in a timely manner

   Strongly disagree ○○○○ Strongly Agree

4. When you were confused about a topic in this class, your peers were helpful

   Strongly disagree ○○○○ Strongly Agree

5. I feel comfortable interacting with my teachers

Strongly disagree ○○○○ Strongly Agree

6. Graduation requirements is clear to me

Strongly disagree ○○○○ Strongly Agree

7. My learning preference

○ Lecture   ○ Hands on activities   ○ Small Group Work

○ Individual Learner

8. My academic strength

○ Math   ○ Science   ○ History   ○ English

○ Other_____

9. My academic weakness

○ Math   ○ Science   ○ History   ○ English

○ Other_____

10. This course was over all beneficial to me

Strongly disagree ○○○○ Strongly Agree

11. Gender

○ Male   ○ Female

12. Ethnicty

○ Asian   ○ Black   ○ White   ○ Latino/Hispanic

○ Multi-Racial   ○ Native American   ○ Other_____

13. Age

○ Under 13   ○ 13   ○ 14   ○ 15   ○ 16 plus

APPENDIX E

DATA DRIVEN COURSE INFORMATION

Grades 9-11 Honors Science Courses

Honors Science2	Honors Science	Count of Student Name	%
Honors Science2	CHEM HNRS	9	21.43%
	ECO HNRS	2	4.76%
	ENV BIO HON	5	11.90%
	ENV/CELL BIO HNRS	6	14.29%
	GEOLO HNRS	2	4.76%
	PHYSICS HNRS	1	2.38%
Honors Science2 Total		**25**	**59.52%**

DID NOT ENROLL IN Honors SCI	(blank)	17	40.48%
DID NOT ENROLL IN Honors SCI Total		**17**	**40.48%**
Grand Total		42	100.00%
Honors Math Courses			

Grades 9-11 Honors Math Courses

Honors Math2	Honors Math	Count of Student Name	%
MATH HONORS	ALG 2 HONORS	5	11.90%
	ALG 3 HONORS	2	4.76%
	GEOM HONORS	4	9.52%
MATH HONORS Total		**11**	**26.19%**

NOT ENROLLED IN MATH HONORS	(blank)	31	73.81%
NOT ENROLLED IN MATH HONORS Total		**31**	**73.81%**
Grand Total		42	100.00%

Grades 9-11 Honors English Courses

Honors English2	Honors English	Count of Student Name	%
Honors English2	AMLIT/COM HON	5	11.90%
	BRIT LIT HNRS	2	4.76%
	FNLIT/COM HON	8	19.05%
DID NOT ENROLL IN HONORS Eng	(blank)	27	64.29%
Grand Total		42	100.00%

Made in the USA
Columbia, SC
18 September 2017